D1613576

John Pope-Hennessy: A BIBLIOGRAPHY

John Pope-Hennessy

by Cecil Beaton

John Pope-Hennessy
A BIBLIOGRAPHY

Compiled by Everett Fahy
With a Foreword by John Russell

The Metropolitan Museum of Art
The Ecco Press

NEW YORK

PUBLISHED BY

The Metropolitan Museum of Art, New York, and
The Ecco Press, New York

Bradford D. Kelleher, *Publisher, The Metropolitan Museum of Art*
John P. O'Neill, *Editor in Chief*
Barbara Burn, *Project Supervisor*
Jean Wagner and Lucy O'Brien, *Editors*
Peter Oldenburg, *Designer*

LIBRARY OF CONGRESS CATALOGING-IN-PUBLICATION DATA
Fahy, Everett.
  John Pope-Hennessy: a bibliography.
  1. Pope-Hennessy, John Wyndham, Sir, 1913–   —
Bibliography. l. Title.
Z8704.18.F33 1986 [N7483.P66]   016.7   86–2503

ISBN 0–87099–469–7 (MMA)
ISBN 0–88001–128–9 (Ecco)

Foreword

BIBLIOGRAPHIES make dull reading, some people say, but I have never found them so. They remind us, they prompt us, and they correct us. They double and treble as history, as biography, and as a freshet of surprises. They reveal the public self, the private self, and the buried self of the person commemorated. How should we not enjoy them, and be grateful to the devoted student who has done the compiling?

A bibliography is the more welcome when its subject has led so active a public life, and published so many books that lasted so well, whereas his occasional writings have for the most part vanished from view (though not from memory). That is the case with John Pope-Hennessy, whose far-scattered articles and reviews may almost be said to constitute a clandestine autobiography. That they should be put in order, and listed, and eventually republished in one form or another, may be a project that he himself would do nothing to advance. But what Everett Fahy has begun with a four-years' labor should have its sequel, for this is a case in which the buried self, the public self, and the private self need to walk side by side.

It was a happy day for New York when the Metropolitan Museum and the Institute of Fine Arts persuaded John Pope-Hennessy to come to their city with a double-headed appointment as Consultative Chairman of the Department of European Paintings at the Met and professor of art history at the Institute. That appointment took effect on January 1, 1977, and New York has been the livelier ever since for

1

the omnipresence of that elongated silhouette, those restless, highly energized movements, and that unmistakable swooping utterance.

J. P.-H. at that time had already had several careers in one. His first book, on Giovanni di Paolo, came out in 1937, when he was twenty-three. His second book, on Sassetta, came out two years later, when he was twenty-five. They ruffled some elderly feathers by their fearless maneuvering on terrain staked out many years earlier by Bernard Berenson, and J. P.-H. himself came to think that he was operating on "a dangerously narrow front." But the unfeigned aplomb, the apparent ease of statement, and the radical character of the investigations made it clear that this was a new person, in a new time, who would have new conclusions to offer on whatever subject he chose to address. This, if ever, was someone who would write what a character in the novels of Ivy Compton-Burnett describes as "Real books coming out of our heads! And not just printed unkindness to other people's."

Those books did indeed come out, and happily for us they are still coming out, close on fifty years later. If they are not listed in this foreword, it is because anyone who picks up this bibliography is likely to have their titles by heart. There are essential areas of Italian art in which not to have read John Pope-Hennessy is to be an ignoramus. So perhaps we can turn to J. P.-H., servant of the public. He could have had an agreeable and constructive life as an independent scholar. Accountable to no one and free to go where he liked and stay there as long as he wanted, he could have produced as much or as little as pleased him. But when he came down from Oxford, he spent six months at the National Gallery in London, traveled on his own for two years in Europe, and then opted to work in the Victoria and Albert Museum, where he dealt with English portrait miniatures, English watercolors, and the Museum's large holdings of John Constable. His career in the V. & A. was interrupted by World War II, and when he was persuaded to return there in 1945 he agreed to do so on condition that he was assigned to a department of which he knew nothing whatever.

In considering these choices, it is important to remember that, although J. P.-H. has an all-seeing eye for the current state of the world, he is the child, as are we all, of a particular moment in time. Lodged way back in his consciousness is the state, or non-state, of art history in England as it had existed not long before his birth. "In England in the first decade of this century," he once wrote, "art history was an unfamiliar, and almost exclusively academic discipline, its techniques appeared unscientific and its findings seemed provisional, and the temptation was to relapse into a *non possumus* approach to every problem as it arose."

It should also be remembered that in first youth J. P.-H. did not take to Bernard Berenson, as to whom he later revised his opinion. ("I found the whole atmosphere at I Tatti *mondain* and unprofessional," he said in 1982. "One is a great prig at that age.") A national museum, by contrast, offered a middle ground between the solitude of the independent scholar and the give-and-take of teaching, in which the element of oral communication is so demanding as to put the act of writing out of mind. Conceivably, also, J. P.-H. was—as he himself said later—"influenced by the facilities I was myself accorded at the age of eighteen in the Kaiser Friedrich Museum in Berlin. They still seem to me to set a standard of which we today should not fall short." Even with Hitler already on the rampage, a great German museum could foster freedom of enquiry.

European museums were staffed, then as now, by professionals. As is well known, J. P.-H. never had any formal training in art history, felt his way into the subject, never thought of putting in for a Ph.D., and is, in fact, a self-taught scholar. It could have made for a rambling, amateurish turn of mind, and one that would have left him on the fringe of the world that interested him. But, as he once said, "I was born in the middle of the world I was meant to be born in. I was brought up with Italian paintings and a great many Chinese objects, among other things. My parents were friends of, for example, the director of the Victoria and Albert Museum, of collectors, and of many other people interested in art." It is also pertinent that his mother, Dame Una Pope-Hennessy, passed on to him the standards of accuracy and clarity of statement which distinguish her books on the French Revolution, early Chinese jades, and Charles Dickens. As the son of someone who detested slipshod work, J. P.-H. was never in any doubt as to the foundations on which worthwhile history should stand. "It is the inadequacy of the historical backgrounds of many scholars that limits their usefulness as art historians. I was never trained as an art historian, but I was trained as a historian (at Balliol College, Oxford) and a pretty rigorous training it was."

It is also important that the element of so-called chance always seems to have been in his favor, and that he acted upon it with his habitual pertinacity. He himself dates his preoccupation with art history to a moment in 1926 when he was walking along Connecticut Avenue in Washington, D.C., where his father was military attaché at the British Embassy. He stepped aside into a bookstore and came out with Crowe and Cavalcaselle on North Italian painting. At Downside, the Roman Catholic school that he went to in England, his interests were encouraged by the Abbot of Downside, Dom John Chapman, and he collected as prizes the six-volume

History of Painting in Italy by Crowe and Cavalcaselle and Bernard Berenson's *Study and Criticism of Italian Art.*

In 1931, as a schoolboy, he was sent to see Kenneth Clark, who was twenty-eight at the time and became in 1933 the youngest-ever director of the National Gallery in London. Anyone who heard, or has read, J. P.-H.'s address at the memorial service to Lord Clark in London in October 1983 will know that this meeting was an inspired move on the part of Logan Pearsall Smith, the American expatriate writer who had engineered it. With hindsight, we could name three separate counts on which Clark had the best of influences on J. P.-H. There was Clark's ability—manifested in 1939 by his book on Leonardo da Vinci—to present some of the highest and most complex of human achievements in terms that were both lucid and authoritative. There were his exceptional capacities as a museum man. ("At his touch," J. P.-H. said in his memorial address, "the then inert hulk of the National Gallery in London sprang to life.") With these, there were a highly developed sense of the human comedy and a disposition which was defined by J. P.-H. when he said that Kenneth Clark "quite legitimately preferred the company of people who were talented, in no matter what field, to the company of untalented professionals."

Unpredictable encounters of an impersonal sort also played their part in his early career. He well remembers, for instance, the Sunday in 1938 when—hard at work on his book on Sassetta—he drove down to lunch at Ashburnham Place in Kent. He arrived late. Lunch had already begun. He sat down in some embarrassment in his appointed place. He looked up, and what did he see on the wall but an unmistakable Sassetta —a predella panel that is now in the Detroit Institute of Arts. This is the kind of thing that makes us believe that he was

5

indeed born into the middle of the world that he was meant to be in.

When J. P.-H.'s New York appointment was announced in 1976, I summed up his activity before World War II by saying that "he read, he traveled, he looked, he wrote. That's all there was to it." I was wrong, of course. There was much more to it than that. Not only did he read, travel, look, and write, but he listened. He had, beyond a doubt, his own way of setting about his activities. (Asked to account for the choice of a subject for his first book, he said "I looked at the literature of Sienese painters to find which of the artists I liked was in the greatest muddle. The answer was Giovanni di Paolo.") But in the foreword to his *Essays on Italian Sculpture* in 1968, he put his development in a broader and deeper perspective:

> Though art historians, like other people, cherish the illusion of free will, their course is set by forces external to themselves; they are controlled by guardians like those in Eliot's *Cocktail Party*. A concern with attributions was instilled in me by early visits with Evelyn Vavalà to the Accademia in Florence, where one learned to distinguish the chubby children of one artist from the chubby children of another. At Assisi I was admitted by Perkins to the sodality of students of Sienese painting. My books about Italian sculpture grew from seeds sown by Jenö Lanyi before the war, and my interest in small bronzes goes back to lunch-time conversations with Saxl about Riccio's works at Padua. One of my most vivid memories is of reading for the first time at Oxford *Italian Primitives at Yale University*. From the perspective of today it seems to me that I owe more to the constructive discouragement of Offner than to the encouragement of other scholars, with the exception of Berenson, to whom my debt is greater still.

Anyone who follows up the leads in this bibliography will be able to add other, later names to this list. J. P.-H. can be memorably dismissive of art historians and curators who fall short of his own standards, but he is both ardent and tender in defense of those who do not. Only a month or two ago he described how, shortly before World War II, he decided that "it was not only works of art that needed to be looked at in the original, but art historians too, since their results were a projection of their personalities. So for some years I made meeting art historians a secondary occupation."

> When I read *The Development of the Italian Schools of Painting*, I can still recall Van Marle's brainless bonhomie. When I read Max Friedländer, I see a frightened face peering out in 1938 from the grille of a door in the Keithstrasse, and when I read Antal I still hear the sound of his gentle, dogmatic, unpersuasive voice. In the first half of the nineteen thirties art history in England was still synonymous with connoisseurship, but through German and Austrian emigration this situation changed, and the field was enriched by scholars of the calibre of Rudolf Wittkower and Edgar Wind and Johannes Wilde and Otto Paecht. With the advent of the Warburg Institute, the subject took an unprecedented depth, and its director Fritz Saxl was singlehandedly responsible for transforming dilettantish scholars of my generation into professionals. During the war I developed a Platonic relationship with aeroplanes (a useful training in accuracy if nothing else), and the occasions I recall with greatest pleasure are the weekly lunches I had with Saxl in Soho discussing the Renaissance portrait medal and the iconography of Riccio's Paschal Candlestick.

As to that, the readers to whom this bibliography is primarily addressed may well be alert to every nuance. They will have his books on their shelves, and they will know that he has been director of both the Victoria and Albert Museum and the British Museum, and that at one time or another he

7

has seemed to many good judges to be the predestined next director, first of the National Gallery in London and later of the Metropolitan Museum in New York. It would be difficult to name any other man whose name comes so often to mind in relation to four of the greatest museums in the English-speaking world. (I should add that the National Gallery of Art in Washington, D.C., is also believed to have made him what it regarded as a tempting offer.)

But this bibliography is concerned to a large extent with the buried Pope-Hennessy—with the author, that is to say, of articles and reviews which have been coming out in this journal or that for more than fifty years but have rarely been reprinted. There are hundreds of these articles. Not even their author has a complete set of them, and if it had not been for Everett Fahy we should never be able to track them down on demand—all the more so since many of the best among them were written for the *Times Literary Supplement* during the years when contributions to that bastion and epitome of English civilization were never signed.

People sometimes regard writings of that kind as ephemeral, by their very nature. They also see them as insubstantial, by reason of the rapidity of composition that is often called for and the lowering of the intellectual sights to which writing for periodicals is said to lead. The "learned article" is one thing, on this reading, and the ad hoc estimate quite another. It is not a reading that will survive the perusal *in extenso* of the articles listed in this book.

These prove, on the contrary, that the collected occasional writings of half a century and more can act as the light cavalry of ideas—darting this way and that, turning up where and when they are least expected, hoisting the flag of truth and beauty where we most need to see it, and not seldom taking an adversary by surprise and leaving him dead on the ground.

They also prove that J. P.-H. at the age of eighteen was already very much the person he is today. Reviewing Clive Bell's *An Account of French Painting* in *The Downside Review* in 1932, he noted the "high percentage of *marivaudage*, as Mr. Bell would doubtless prefer it termed" which the author had allowed himself. Reviewing Sacheverell Sitwell's short study of Mozart, he called it "strangely out of date" and regretted that the author should have missed both the "extraordinary expansion of the rondo form in the D minor piano concerto" and the way in which the minuet in Mozart's G minor quintet is "at least half way along the road from Haydn to the great minuetto in Brahms's A minor quartet." These are not the attitudes of a beginner.

A day or two after his twentieth birthday he began to write for *The New Statesman and Nation*, which at that time was the leading intellectual weekly in England. I shall forbear to name the study of English painting in which J. P.-H., on December 30, 1933, found all too many "anecdotes selected with an unvarying eye for the irrelevant." (When one of the authors in question was rash enough to write a letter-to-the-editor in reply, J. P.-H. wrote from Balliol to remark that the author seemed to claim for himself "an automatic exemption from the obligation of accuracy and coherence on which a better-educated public might insist.")

One of the privileges of London life in the 1930s was the succession of major winter exhibitions at the Royal Academy. In April 1934, J. P.-H. wrote a review of the English art exhibition there in which he displayed for the first time a gift for concise, forceful, and unhedged summations that last very well. There were not many people in 1934 who would have said of George Stubbs that he was "not primarily a sporting painter," but someone "to whom we can give unstinted admiration." Already firm in his likes and dislikes, he said that "as a painter, Hogarth cannot be over-rated. He has speed and animation, accomplishment and wit." And if there were bad paintings in the show, as there certainly were, J. P.-H. responded to them in a way that shows him to have been already in 1934 what he was to be all his life—a student above all of the creative process. "Even the bad picture is a key to the past," he wrote. "The fault is ours if we refuse to use the lock into which it can be fitted."

Other judgments from the 1930s demand to be lifted from their context, so briskly do they show to what an extent J. P.-H. in first youth was on top of his tasks. In December 1936 he said of Berenson's *Lists* that in 1932 "as now, the book seemed to have achieved an astonishing equipoise between the dangers of over-rigid scholarship and inclusion for the sake of mere inclusiveness." Nor did he hesitate to make judgments that still strike us by their boldness—that Gainsborough's *Drinkstone Park* was "the nearest thing that I know to alchemy in painting," for instance, or that "in many respects, Raphael apart, Seurat is the most remarkable artistic phenomenon there has ever been."

If he did not write often on Italian old master painting, it was doubtless because the subject rarely came up in the context of the London exhibition schedule. (Nobody seems to have asked him to write on the old master exhibitions—some of the greatest things of their kind ever held—that were organized in Venice in the 1930s.) Like everyone else who saw it, he recognized the exhibition of seventeenth-century art at the Royal Academy in the winter of 1937–38 as one of the landmarks of a lifetime. "During the 17th century," he wrote, "the use of oil paint . . . attained a fluency, a subtlety and a strength, on which no advance has been or ever can be made. . . . The art of the 18th and 19th centuries under one aspect is nothing but a struggle to maintain a standard the 17th century had set."

Anyone who feels that I have overstressed the element of combative generalization in J. P.-H.'s occasional writings has only to turn to the series of international surveys of "Recent Research" which he contributed to *The Burlington Magazine* over many years. This was an activity in which an Edwardian *non possumus* was out of the question. Whatever had been written, on no matter what subject, had to be read. Once read, it had to be assessed. The author might be English, American, French, German, Swiss, Italian, Belgian, Dutch, or Spanish. The subject might be close to J. P.-H.'s own particular interests, or it might not. Either way, he went ahead. The pressures of World War II found no reflection in these surveys. Even when he was working full-time in the British Air Ministry, J. P.-H. gave the same unhurried, even-handed treatment to subjects and authors from all over. We may also salute, at a more than forty years' distance, the steadiness of mind with which he wrote, for *Art in America* magazine early in 1943, a stringent and unsentimental account of certain minor works of art relating to Pisa and Siena which were in his possession. No one could possibly have inferred from this that Great Britain and Italy were at war on Italian soil and that the very survival of those two cities was in jeopardy.

By 1943, the state of Europe was such that the authors discussed in "Recent Research" were almost all American, and thereafter there was necessarily a silence until July 1946. When something akin to normal life was resumed, articles came flooding in once more. Up to twenty-eight at a time were summarized and assessed until well into the 1950s—by which time anyone less curious, less energetic, or less conscientious would have long ago turned over the job to someone else. The effect in dark times of these deft and multifarious estimates has not been forgotten.

In the many articles that J. P.-H. contributed to the *Burlington* in those gruesome years, he treated the life of the mind as an international continuum that should be interrupted as little as possible. With France waiting passively for the German invasion, he published an article in the *Gazette des Beaux-Arts* on Georges de la Tour. When England and Italy were at war, he discussed the marbles in the Boboli Gardens as if it were still possible to drop everything and go over to see them. Nor was he forced into inactivity by the starveling visual diet that was available in England between 1940 and the end of the war. He looked, he thought, and he wrote, no matter how thin the pretext might be.

It came as a surprise to many people that when Matisse and Picasso made their reappearance in liberated Paris at the Salon d'Automne in 1944, one of the first English visitors to comment upon it was J. P.-H. Where others were disoriented by the experience, he spoke in particular of a still-life by Matisse "whose rich harmonies and classical structure lend it much of the significance which a middle period Titian would have had for the mannerists of the later cinquecento." He also said that Matisse was "the painting of yesterday, while the vital, often repellent pictures of Picasso are the painting of today." This might have been an isolated response to an altogether exceptional occasion, but in point of fact J. P.-H. knows more about what is going on in the world of new art than almost anyone among his contemporaries.

He has also had, on occasion, an exemplary patience with writers whose approach to great art is unprofessional. "Non-professional" might be a better adjective for Adrian Stokes, the English aesthetician who published a book on Venice in 1945. There were those in the profession who dismissed it out of hand. J. P.-H. was not among them. Admittedly, he wrote that "One would judge Mr. Stokes to be almost entirely deficient in the gifts required on the one hand for constructive aesthetic thinking and on the other for original professional study. He has neither a respect for logic nor a capacity for logical expression." "But," he went on, "he possesses intuitions in their way as important as any of these—intuitions which might, if left to themselves, make him the most vital, the most delightful and perhaps the most significant contemporary esthetic commentator. He can write, and he can feel." Sharper by far was his dismissal of an Italian colleague, around the same time, for having produced "a thrice-refined pabulum of transcendental moonshine."

As will by now be clear, J. P.-H. has at no time in his career been "a specialist" in the narrow, confining, almost fortified sense of the word. There was a time, for instance, when his chief academic interest was Dark Age and Carolingian history. "So strong was it," he wrote recently, "that when I first went to Milan in 1933, my prime objective was the treasury at Monza (with the baskets in which Theolinda thought the loaves and fishes had been distributed) not the Brera Gallery or Leonardo's *Last Supper*." This was the stage in his life at which the free-thinking readers of *The New Statesman and Nation* learned from J. P.-H. that "The ninth century was a period of transition. Its Alcuins, its Theodulfs, its Walafrids sound the death-rattle of a classicism garrotted by St. Gregory." "Was it a matter for regret?" he went on to ask, and we may wonder how many of his readers were competent to reply.

After World War II it was in conversation, more often than in print, that he manifested his gift for the concise plain statement that lands where we least expect it. Readers did however glimpse it from time to time—as when he wrote in

1945 of the period (during the heyday of Turner and Constable) when "the center of gravity of western painting was in London and not in Paris or Rome or Madrid." More provocative than many an hour-long seminar was his thirteen-word reference in 1950 to "Holbein as he was, earnest, fertile and humane, in all his mysterious complexity." In 1952 he suggested that "modern painting began in May 1432, when the *Adoration of the Lamb* was set up in Ghent—the first work in which the retinal reactions of the artist to perceived reality are recognisably our own." In 1953 we treasured especially a passage in his review of the exhibition of Lorenzo Lotto in Venice: "How strange . . . that the patrons of Titian and Palma Vecchio should not have welcomed with enthusiasm those glazed figures wrapped in printed paper, those angels with green hair, those saints with electric-blue boots advancing resolutely from their frames!"

Even so, people persisted in trying to pin him down, although he sometimes gave them the slip with an allusion that not every professional would recognize. (That Tintoretto around 1580 reminded him of "angle shots by a Cinquecento Carol Reed" was one such.) Meanwhile, international recognition came. When J. P.-H. was in his early thirties, Roberto Longhi had this to say about his studies of Sienese painting: "Il Pope-Hennessy nel suo recente libro sul maestro (Sassetta) ha finalmente avuto la decisione di rilevarne i molti e precoci fiorentinismi, togliendolo così da quell' atmosfera pseudo-buddistica in cui lo avevano lasciato gli studi decadentisti precedenti."

But, even as that was being written, J. P.-H. was reminding his readers that "Were a poll to be taken of the six most beautiful paintings in the world, the Vienna Vermeer would surely find a place on every list." And in 1975 he said of the *Three Ages of Man* by Titian, now on long loan to the National

Gallery of Scotland, that "I would rather own this painting than any other picture in the world. . . . The pragmatism of the 'Georgics', the mythology of the 'Metamorphoses', the philosophy of the 'De Rerum Naturae'—these and much else lay below the surface of Titian's consciousness."

These divergences from specialization notwithstanding, J. P.-H. has always known when to concentrate, and he has also always known that concentration means having the original works of art near at hand. "You can't study sculpture from photographs," he told two visitors from Rutgers University in 1981. "The only way to study sculpture is to touch it, see how deep the cutting is, the exact nature of the modeling, and all that sort of thing. The precondition of everything that I have written about sculpture was to live, day in, day out, for twenty-two years with a collection of Italian sculpture and a very large cast collection."

Yet concentration and specialization are two different things. "I benefited very greatly," he said not long ago, "at the Victoria & Albert and at the British Museum from the obligation to get on terms with unfamiliar media and cultures and areas of study; one learned to take Victorian brass lecterns and filthy plastic bags containing the mummies of Peruvian children in one's stride."

Though now relieved of that particular obligation, J. P.-H. is as reluctant as ever to stick with what he already knows. The logbook of a recent two-week motor-journey in France gives some indication of this. Having traveled relatively little in France, J. P.-H. was determined to correct that lacuna. Day by day, the tally mounted. Goya in Agen and Castres, Romanesque architecture in Souillac and Conques and Moissac, the burial place of Saint Thomas Aquinas in Toulouse, Ingres in Montauban, the Musée Stendhal in Grenoble, Toulouse-Lautrec in Albi, Domenichino in Béziers, Courbet in Montpellier, the Maison Carrée in Nîmes, Laurana in Avignon and Marseilles, the *Coronation of the Virgin* in Villeneuve-lès-Avignon, a fake Donatello in the Lapidary Museum in Avignon, Rubens in the cathedral in Grasse, Uccello in Chambéry, and the basilica of Saint-Maximin-la-Sainte-Baume, where Mary Magdalen is buried—all these and much else were scrutinized. As a rare concession to the concept of "relaxation," J. P.-H. spent one afternoon in Arles in front of a television set, watching the finals of a lawn-tennis tournament.

As in much else that J. P.-H. does, there was something in all this of Bernard Berenson in his capacity as reader, sightseer, and cross-cultural mediator. The Berenson who had read everything, looked at everything, been everywhere, and talked to everyone is not a stranger to the subject of this bibliography, either as a human being or as an exemplar. Throughout his very long lifetime, Berenson was a controversial figure—adulated by some, detested by others. (J. P.-H. first heard of him when his mother took him to tea with Helen Clay Frick in the summer of 1927, and Miss Frick happened to say "Berenson. Never let me hear the man's name again.") Alike in conversation and in print, he heard the arguments for and against B. B. over and over again.

And then, from 1945 onwards, he and B. B. became friends. In his own words, "I owe more to this association than to any other professional relationship. . . . The most important thing I learned was that a stable system of value judgments was the tent pole of art history."

Many items in this bibliography bear witness to his feelings for B. B. Together, they constitute an elegy none the less poignant for the informality of its presentation and its dispersal among articles now not easy to come by. I think especially of the review, dated August 28th, 1953, of the new edition of Berenson's *Venetian Painters of the Renaissance*, first published fifty-nine years earlier. As in his own work, J. P.-H. takes the emphasis away from the historian and directs it toward the work of art. "The last word," he said, "rests with the work of art, and ultimately it is the work of art that passes a favorable verdict upon Mr. Berenson, and an unfavorable verdict upon writers whose esthetic judgment operates on a more superficial plane."

Unlike certain other people, on the other hand, J. P.-H. has taken care to differentiate himself from Berenson, much as he admires the intellectual energy that prompted B. B. to say, when he was eighty-eight, that he would be prepared to make a new edition of the Florentine lists on condition that he could take every decision about an attribution as if he had never taken it before. This is what J. P.-H. said in 1981:

> Berenson declared on more than one occasion that almost everything that he had published was written from the standpoint of the consumer, the person who looks at works of art. My own bias is the opposite; I try to look at works of art from the standpoint of the producer, to understand the way in which the work of art developed and why it took the form it did. With the study of Italian sculpture there is no second option. So long as it remains a matter of comparing one finished sculpture with another, all solutions are approximate. The valid comparison is not between two finished sculptures but between the processes by which they were produced.

As between J. P.-H. and Bernard Berenson, we are entitled to point to another difference. B. B. did his work in the field, on the hoof. When he came back, it was to his own library. He never taught. He never worked in a museum. He never organized, catalogued, or installed an exhibition. J. P.-H. has done all these things, and he has done them in such a way that his work in retrospect seems to have been all of a piece. In recent years, his books on Luca della Robbia and Benvenuto Cellini have spoken for him, but so has the reinstallation of the European Paintings galleries at the Metropolitan Museum, where every least label seems to bear his mark.

He has done the work of a connoisseur, a detective, a moralist, and a teacher. There have been occasional pieces, like the examination of Roger Fry's record at the Metropolitan Museum, in which he has set history to rights in ways that called for the narrative skills of novelist and biographer. And there was his account of the exact state of affairs in Florence not long after the catastrophic flood of 1966, in which an apparently impartial auditing had overtones of Daniel Defoe's *Journal of the Plague Year*. Yet how many of those who pick up this bibliography will know where to find the one, or in which issue of the London *Financial Times* to look for the other? At those times, and on many another occasion here recorded, J. P.-H. was the necessary human being who said what had to be said. And that is what makes this, in its turn, a necessary book.

JOHN RUSSELL

Acknowledgments

FOUR YEARS AGO, when it seemed that a bibliography would be an appropriate tribute for Sir John Pope-Hennessy's seventieth birthday, I little knew how much time it would take to compile. I assumed I could do it in a few weeks: just several visits to the library and perhaps a few letters to colleagues in Europe. But long before December 13, 1983, I realized that my plan was unrealistic. I had underestimated the number and the variety of Sir John's publications. Whenever I thought that I had found everything, new material appeared. And it keeps on turning up as we go to press.

For help with sources in New York I relied on Theodora Ashmead. For information about reviews in English newspapers, I am indebted to Geoffrey Ashton and Gordon Phillips. Erich Schleier, Michel Laclotte, Gail Solberg, Michael Mallon, Yvonne Hackenbroch, and Richmond Crinkley provided valuable information.

The Robert Lehman Foundation helped defray the cost of the preparation of the manuscript.

The 556 items listed here are arranged chronologically. Books appear first, followed by articles listed alphabetically, first by the publication in which they appear and then by the first significant word of the title. Book reviews appear alphabetically by the name of the author, and exhibition reviews are arranged alphabetically by city. These are followed by occasional pieces such as introductions to other writers' books, letters-to-the-editor, and obituaries.

From the very start John Russell has encouraged this project, and to him I am grateful for the delightful essay that serves as a foreword.

EVERETT FAHY

Bibliography

1932

"*Maria Edgeworth: Chosen Letters* edited by F. V. Barry." *The Downside Review* 50: 143–45.

"*Bath* by Edith Sitwell." *The Downside Review* 50: 537–38.

"*Mozart* by Sacheverell Sitwell." *The Downside Review* 50: 534–36.

"The French Exhibition: Introductions in Retrospect." Review of *An Account of French Painting* by Clive Bell, *A Short History of French Painting* by Eric G. Underwood, and *An Outline of French Painting* by R. H. Wilenski. *The Downside Review* 50: 253–62.

1933

"*The Art of Henri Matisse* by Albert C. Barnes and Violette de Mazia." *The Downside Review* 51: 561–65.

"*The Book of Talbot* by Violet Clifton." *The Downside Review* 51: 570–72.

"*A Half-Day's Ride* by Padraic Colum." *Blackfriars* 14 (January): 66.

"*Artists at Work* by Stanley Casson." *Blackfriars* 14 (June): 517–19.

"*Romanesque Architecture* by F. Eygum." *Blackfriars* 14 (January): 66.

"Mr. Roger Fry on French Art." Review of *Characteristics of French Art* by Roger Fry. *Blackfriars* 14 (March): 221–23.

"*Park* by John Gray." *Blackfriars* 14 (January): 64–66.

21

"The Graeco-Roman Influence." Review of *Raphael* by Charles Holmes. *The New Statesman and Nation*, June 3: 738–39.

"*Raphael* by Charles Holmes." *The Downside Review* 51: 565–66.

"*Domenicos Theotocopulos—El Greco* by Achilleus Kyrae." *Blackfriars* 14 (June): 515–17.

"*Rhythmic Form in Art* by A. Richter." *Blackfriars* 14 (April): 329–31.

"English Painting." Review of *English Painting* by R. H. Wilenski, *An Introduction to English Painting* by John Rothenstein, *A Short History of English Painting* by Eric G. Underwood, and *A Short History of Painting in England* by Miles F. de Montmorency. *The New Statesman and Nation*, December 30: 874–75.

"Recent Art Exhibitions." Review of work by Barbara Hepworth and Ben Nicholson at Tooth, watercolors by Paul Nash and landscapes by Ethelbert White at Leicester Galleries, and the New English Art Club exhibition at the New Burlington Galleries, London. *Blackfriars* 14 (January): 68–72.

"Recent Art Exhibitions." Review of an exhibition at the Royal Academy of the work of 14 recently deceased Royal Academicians, including Dicksee, Davies, Sims, Orpen, Ricketts, and Muirhead. *Blackfriars* 14 (February) 156–58.

"Recent Art Exhibitions." Review of the William Orpen exhibition at the Royal Academy and the exhibitions of etchings by Augustus John and Dunoyer de Segonzac at Leicester Galleries. *Blackfriars* 14 (March): 233–37.

"Recent Art Exhibitions." Review of the Elizabethan exhibition at Grosvenor Place and Three French Reigns, an exhibition organized by Sir Philip Sassoon. *Blackfriars* 14 (May): 430–33.

"Recent Art Exhibitions." Review of the Jacob Epstein exhibition at Leicester Galleries and the summer exhibition at the Royal Academy. *Blackfriars* 14 (June): 519–22.

"Recent Art Exhibitions." Review of the Henri Matisse exhibition at Tooth, the Max Ernst exhibition at Mayor Gallery, the Duncan Grant exhibition at Agnew's, and the Industrial Art exhibition at Dorland House. *Blackfriars* 14 (August): 698–701.

"Recent Art Exhibitions." Review of an exhibition at Mayor Gallery mounted to complement Herbert Read's *In Art Now*. *Blackfriars* 14 (November): 968–70.

1934

"*Leonardo da Vinci, the Artist* by Edward McCurdy." *The Downside Review* 52: 343–44.

"*Picasso et ses amis* by Fernande Olivier." *Blackfriars* 15 (April): 294–95.

"*Stones of Rimini* by Adrian Stokes." *Blackfriars* 15 (June): 434–35.

"Art Chronicle." Review of *A Short History of English Painting* by Eric G. Underwood, *An Outline of English Painting* by R. H. Wilenski, and an essay on English art by Herbert Read in the December 1933 *Burlington Magazine*. *Blackfriars* 15 (February): 159–63.

"The English Exhibition." Review of an exhibition held at Burlington House, London. *The Dublin Review*, April: 222–36.

"English Painting." Letter in response to one from Eric G. Underwood concerning the review of his book, *A Short History of English Painting*. *The New Statesman and Nation*, January 27: 116.

1935

"Cloister Art." Review of *Carolingian Art* by Roger Hinks. *The New Statesman and Nation*, May 4: 648.

1936

"*Paul Cézanne* by Gerstle Mack." *The Burlington Magazine* 68 (March): 151–52.

"A Welcome Prototype." Review of *The Iconography of the First Duke of Wellington* by Lord Gerald Wellesley and John Steegman. *The New Statesman and Nation*, February 1: 160.

"*I Pittori italiani del Rinascimento* by Bernard Berenson. *Pitture italiane del Rinascimento* by Bernard Berenson." *The Burlington Magazine* 69 (December): 287–88.

"The Gainsborough Exhibition." Review of an exhibition at 45 Park Lane, London. *The New Statesman and Nation*, February 29: 307.

"French Painting in the Nineteenth Century." Review of an exhibition at the New Burlington Galleries, London. *The Tablet*, October 24: 566–68.

"Masters of French 19th Century Painting." Review of an exhibition at the New Burlington Galleries, London. *The Burlington Magazine* 69 (November): 222–25.

"Masters of French Nineteenth Century Painting." Letter in response to one from W. W. Winkworth. *The Burlington Magazine* 69 (December): 287.

1937

Giovanni di Paolo, 1403–1483. London: Chatto & Windus. xiv, 194 pages, 32 plates.

"A Predella Panel by Giovanni di Paolo." *The Burlington Magazine* 71 (September): 108–9.

"Recent Research." Review of periodical articles by L. Coletti on the Mostra Giottesca, R. Buscaroli on Melozzo da Forlì, L. Becherucci on Cimabue, G. Pudelko on Antonio Vivarini,

W. R. Valentiner on frescoes in Palazzo Sclafani at Palermo, L. Müntz on Barent Fabritius, E. P. Richardson on Hoogstraten, A. Staring on Taco Scheltema, W. Schöne on Flemish painting, and others. *The Burlington Magazine* 71 (December): 290–91.

"An Exhibition of English Painting." Review of an exhibition at Agnew's, London. *The Burlington Magazine* 70 (June): 296–99.

"Sir Joshua Reynolds." Review of an exhibition at 45 Park Lane, London. *The Listener*, February 17: 302.

"Paul Nash." Review of an exhibition at the Redfern Gallery, London. *The Listener*, May 12: 918–19.

1938

"A Group of Studies by Luca Carlevarijs." *The Burlington Magazine* 73 (September): 126–31.

"A Passion Predella by Sassetta." *The Burlington Magazine* 73 (August): 49–50.

"Zacchia il Vecchio and Lorenzo Zacchia." *The Burlington Magazine* 72 (May): 213–23.

"*Venetian Painters* by F. J. Mather, Jr." *The Burlington Magazine* 72 (February): 97.

"*Contemporary British Painters* by Paul Nash." *The Burlington Magazine* 72 (May): 250.

"*Lorenzo di Pietro detto il Vecchietta* by Giorgio Vigni." *The Burlington Magazine* 73 (November): 228.

"Recent Research." Review of periodical articles by M. C. Ferrari on Neri da Rimini, W. R. Valentiner on Andrea dell' Aquila and the Master of the Castello Nativity, P. Bacci on Vecchietta, E. Panofsky and G. Pudelko on Piero di Cosimo, E. Möller on Leonardo, P. della Pergola on Francesco Mochi, E. Wiegand on 15th-century German sculpture, J. Sommer on Johann Koerbecke, A. C. M. Mensing on Dirk Crabeth, G.

Isarlo on Le Nain, J. Rewald on Courture's pupil Achille Emperaire, and others. *The Burlington Magazine* 73 (September): 132–34.

"Seventeenth-Century Art at Burlington House." *The Tablet,* January 15: 74.

"Neapolitan Painting, 1600–1900." Review of the Mostra della Pittura napoletana at Castel Nuovo, Naples. *The Burlington Magazine* 73 (August): 82–85.

"Giovanni di Paolo." Letter in response to a review by Langton Douglas. *The Burlington Magazine* 72 (February): 95.

1939

Sassetta. London: Chatto & Windus. 239 pages, 32 plates.

"Francesco di Giorgio, Neroccio: Two Madonnas and an Altarpiece." *The Burlington Magazine* 75 (December): 229–35.

"Notes on Andrea Vanni." *The Burlington Magazine* 74 (February): 92–97.

"The Panel Paintings of Pellegrino di Mariano." *The Burlington Magazine* 74 (May): 213–18.

"*Dipinti inediti e sconosciuti di Pietro Lorenzetti, Bernardo Daddi, etc. in Siena e nel contado* by Péleo Bacci." *The Burlington Magazine* 75 (December): 250–51.

"*Melozzo da Forlì* by Rezio Buscaroli." *The Burlington Magazine* 74 (January): 45.

"*The Life and Works of Colvin Smith, R. S. A.* by R. C. M. Colvin-Smith." *The Burlington Magazine* 75 (August): 92.

"Recent Research." Review of periodical articles by G. Bottai on Italian art policy, H. Swarzenski on William de Brailes, P. Metz on Arnolfo di Cambio, G. Vigni on Grosseto cathedral, C. Botto on S. Trinita in Florence, U. Middeldorf on Francesco da Sangallo, O. Giglioli on Pier Francesco Toschi, S. Bottari on Filippo Palladino, E. Tietze on Titian, G. Fiocco on Tiepolo,

W. R. Valentiner on Isaac Luttichuys, E. P. Richardson on Brueghel and van Goyen, J. Billioud on Françoise Duparc, E. S. King on Delacroix, and others. *The Burlington Magazine* 74 (January): 33–34.

"Recent Research." Review of periodical articles by C. Brandi on Giotto, M. Salmi on Pisa cathedral, G. Marchini on Giotto, W. Cohn-Goerke on Agostino di Giovanni and Agnolo di Ventura, F. J. Mather on Lorenzo Lotto, K. Steinbart on Pontormo, P. Wescher on Heemskerk and Scorel, M. C. Benedict on Osias Beert, E. P. Richardson on Frans van Mieris, R. C. Smith on Frans Post, R. Baum on Rowlandson and Avercamp, E. P. Richardson on Eicholtz, R. Jullian on Puvis de Chavannes, A. Neumeyer on Marées, and others. *The Burlington Magazine* 74 (April): 196–98.

"Recent Research." Review of periodical articles by M. Weinberger on a 13th-century fresco at Montepiano, E. Vavalà on a cross close to the Bigallo crucifix, A. Péter on Simone Martini, C. Gnudi on Andrea da Fiesole, A. Weller on Francesco di Giorgio, E. Möller on Leonardo, A. L. Mayer on Titian, R. Gallo on Veronese, E. P. Richardson on Rogier van der Weyden, A. Bredius on Carel Fabritius, R. Tolman on Malbone, J. W. Lane on Bonington, K. Leonhardi on Joseph Anton Koch, and others. *The Burlington Magazine* 75 (September): 128–30.

"The Royal Academy Exhibition of Scottish Art." *The Burlington Magazine* 74 (February): 67–71.

"A Jacopo della Quercia Exhibition." Review of the commemorative exhibition of the 15th-century Sienese sculptor held at the Palazzo Publico, Siena. *The Burlington Magazine* 74 (January): 36.

"A Pordenone Exhibition." Review of the Mostra del Pordenone e della pittura friulana del Rinascimento at the Museo Civico, Udine. *The Burlington Magazine* 75 (August): 78–83.

"Sassetta." Letter in response to a review by Langton Douglas. *The Burlington Magazine* 75 (October): 155.

1940

"Beccafumi in the Victoria and Albert Museum." *The Burlington Magazine* 76 (April): 110–23.

"Luca Carlevarijs: Some Unpublished Drawings." *The Burlington Magazine* 77 (July): 27–31.

"An Unpublished Painting by Delacroix." *The Burlington Magazine* 77 (September): 88.

"*Giovanni Antonio Pordenone* by Giuseppe Fiocco." *The Burlington Magazine* 76 (February): 66.

"Recent Research." Review of periodical articles by S. Ameisenowa on the Master of the St. George Codex, W. Cohn-Goerke on 14th-century Sienese sculpture and Giovanni d'Agostino, E. Vavalà on Agnolo Gaddi and Lorenzo Monaco, G. Nicodemi on Romanino, G. Fiocco on Moretto, A. Morassi on Foppa, C. Gamba on Savoldo, N. Beets on Cornelius Anthonisz, A. Bredius on Rembrandt, R. Longhi on Eberhard Keil, C. Bassi on Gian Pietro Ligari, H. W. Williams on Guardi, P. Jamot on Georges de la Tour, and others. *The Burlington Magazine* 76 (January): 28–32.

"Recent Research." Review of periodical articles by E. Vavalà and R. Longhi on Niccolò di Pietro, E. S. King on Antonio Vivarini, H. Tietze and E. Tietze-Conrat on Domenico Campagnola, W. Suida and H. Tietze on Titian, E. Tietze-Conrat and H. B. Wehle on Tintoretto, H. S. Francis on Jacopo Bassano, W. R. Valentiner on Wilhelm Drost, A. Pigler on iconography, and others. *The Burlington Magazine* 76 (April): 132–36.

"Recent Research." Review of periodical articles by P. Cellini on Nicola di Nuto, G. de Francovich on Arnolfo di Cambio, U. Middeldorf on Luca della Robbia and Desiderio, W. R. Valentiner on Michelozzo and Ghiberti, F. Kriegbaum on Benvenuto Cellini, P. Rimington on Battista Lorenzi, and others. *The Burlington Magazine* 77 (December): 201–2.

1941

"Donatello Reinterpreted." Review of *Donatello*, a picture book published by the Phaidon Press. *The Listener*, July 17: 94.

"The Greatest English Portrait Painter." Review of *Reynolds* by E. K. Waterhouse. *The Listener*, August 14: 239.

1942

"*The Agony in the Garden.*" On Giovanni Bellini's painting in the National Gallery. *The Listener*, September 17: 367.

"The Hampton Court Collection." Survey of the pictures on view at Hampton Court Palace. *The Listener*, September 3: 303.

"*St. George and the Dragon.*" On Tintoretto's painting in the National Gallery. *The Listener*, July 9: 45.

"Art History and Psychology." Review of *On Art and Connoisseurship* by Max J. Friedländer. *The Listener*, August 6: 180–81.

"Flemish Drawings." Review of *Flemish Drawings at Windsor Castle* by Leo van Puyvelde. *The Listener*, November 26: 687.

"The Art of Portrait Painting." Review of *Frans Hals* by N. S. Trivas. *The Listener*, April 23: 527.

"Recent Research." Review of periodical articles by C. Kuhn on Hermann Scheere, O. Pächt on Jean Fouquet, R. Kennedy on Baldovinetti, M. Meiss on Piero della Francesca, G. M. Richter on Fra Carnevale, G. H. Edgell on Piero della Francesca, W. R. Valentiner on Leonardo and Verrocchio, C. de Tolnay on Michelangelo, A. Heppner on Brouwer and Rembrandt, W. Stechow on Rembrandt, G. van Muyden on Arlaud and Largillière, F. Mauroner on Gianfrancesco Costa, A. Ritchie on Ingres, L. Burroughs on Degas, H. Marceau and D. Rosen on Daumier, and others. *The Burlington Magazine* 80 (January): 24–26.

1943

"Bellini's 'Doge.'" On Giovanni Bellini's portrait of Leonardo Loredano in the National Gallery. *The Listener*, May 27: 636.

"A Madonna by Andrea Vanni." *The Burlington Magazine* 83 (July): 174–77.

"Nicholas Hilliard and Mannerist Art Theory." *Journal of the Warburg and Courtauld Institutes* 6: 89–100.

"A Predella Panel by Masolino." *The Burlington Magazine* 82 (February): 30–31.

"Some Aspects of the Cinquecento in Siena." Discussion of paintings and drawings in the author's collection. *Art in America* 31 (April): 63–77.

"Recent Research." Review of periodical articles by G. Swarzenski on Donatello, R. G. Mather on Michelozzo, L. M. Bongiorno on Silvestro dell'Aquila, W. R. Valentiner on Francesco di Giorgio and Laurana, C. Gilbert on Piero della Francesca, G. M. Richter on Giorgione, M. Cutter on Caravaggio, E. P. Richardson on Renieri, Saraceni and Caravaggio, W. G. Constable and L. van Puyvelde on Rubens, A. C. Sewter on Haydon, and others. *The Burlington Magazine* 83 (September): 231–33.

"Drawings from the Witt Collection." Review of an exhibition of Old Master drawings at the Victoria and Albert Museum, London. *The Burlington Magazine* 82 (April): 103.

"Old Master Drawings." Review of an exhibition at the Victoria and Albert Museum, London. *The Listener*, February 11: 175.

1944

Paolo Uccello: The Rout of San Romano in the National Gallery, London. The Gallery Books no. 4. London: Percy Lund Humphries & Company Ltd. 24 pages, 17 figures.

"The Development of Realistic Painting in Siena." Parts 1, 2. *The Burlington Magazine* 84 (May, June): 110–19, 139–44.

"Dutch Drawings at Windsor Castle." Review of *Dutch Drawings at Windsor Castle* by Leo van Puyvelde. *The Listener*, June 1: 610.

"The Autumn Salon." Review of the Salon d'Automne in Paris. *The Listener*, November 2: 494–95.

1945

"The English Tradition of Painting." *The Listener*, April 19: 431–32.

"Nicholas Hilliard and Mannerist Art Theory." In *England and the Mediterranean Tradition: Studies in Art, History and Literature*: 69–80. London: Oxford University Press. Reprinted from the *Journal of the Warburg and Courtauld Institutes*, 1943.

"Holbein's Drawings at Windsor Castle." Review of *Holbein's Drawings at Windsor Castle* edited by K. T. Parker. *The Listener*, June 14: 664.

"*Venice: An Aspect of Art* by Adrian Stokes." *The Listener*, September 6: 273–74.

"Seventeenth-Century Dutch Painting." Review of an exhibition in London sponsored by the Arts Council of Great Britain. *The Listener*, August 9: 157.

1946

Sandro Botticelli: The Nativity in the National Gallery, London. The Gallery Books no. 15. London: Percy Lund Humphries & Company Ltd. 24 pages, 16 figures.

"Barna, the Pseudo-Barna and Giovanni d'Asciano." *The Burlington Magazine* 88 (February): 35–37.

"A Painting by Peruzzi." *The Burlington Magazine* 88 (October): 237–41.

"Two Portraits by Domenichino." *The Burlington Magazine* 88 (August): 186–91.

"The Romano Foundation, Florence." Review of a collection of sculpture formed by Salvatore Romano and catalogued by Luisa Becherucci. *The Burlington Magazine* 88 (November): 276–79.

"Northern Renaissance Art." Review of *The Art of the Renaissance in Northern Europe* by Otto Benesch. *The Listener,* August 15: 220.

"*Capolavori dell'arte senese* edited by Enzo Carli." Review of the commemorative catalogue of an exhibition held at Siena, 1944/45. *The Burlington Magazine* 88 (December): 316–17.

"*Yankee Stonecutters* by Albert Teneyck Gardner." *The Burlington Magazine* 88 (September): 234.

"*Fragonard: Drawings for Ariosto* edited by Philip Hofer, Elizabeth Mongan and Jean Seznec." *The Listener,* July 11: 57.

" 'Mad Margot.' " Review of *Pieter Bruegel the Elder: The Dulle Griet* by Leo van Puyvelde. *The Listener,* April 11: 484.

"*Aristide Maillol, 1861–1944* edited by Andrew C. Ritchie." *The Burlington Magazine* 88 (January): 25.

"*The Faber Gallery, Florentine Paintings: Fifteenth Century* by Kenneth Clark. *Music in Painting* by Lawrence Haward. *Blake* by Geoffrey Keynes. *Degas* by R. H. Wilenski." *The Burlington Magazine* 88 (March): 78.

"*Antonio del Pollajuolo* by Giovanni Colacicchi and *Antonio e Piero del Pollajuolo* by Attilio Sabatini." *The Burlington Magazine* 88 (July): 180–81.

"*Paolo Veronese: 'The Family of Darius before Alexander'* by Simon

Harcourt-Smith and *Georges Seurat: 'Une Baignade, Asnieres'* by Douglas Cooper." *The Listener*, February 28: 281–82.

"Recent Research." Review of periodical articles by A. Graziani on the Master of the Fogg Pietà, E. Carli on Giovanni di Balduccio, F. J. Mather on Masaccio, R. Longhi on Masolino and Masaccio, E. Carli on Abruzzese painting, L. M. Bongiorno on sculpture at Aquila, U. Middeldorf on Agostino di Duccio, W. R. Valentiner on Mino da Fiesole, M. Pease on Carpaccio, F. R. Shapley on a portrait of Francesco Sforza, W. R. Suida on Andrea Solario, C. Gilbert on Savoldo, E. Tietze-Conrat on Titian, W. R. Suida on Veronese, M. Weinberger on Ammanati, and others. *The Burlington Magazine* 88 (July): 172–75.

"Recent Research." Review of periodical articles by M. J. Friedländer on Memling, Rogier van der Weyden and Cornelis van Cleve, C. de Tolnay on Hugo van der Goes and Bosch, E. S. King on the Master of the Joseph Legend, W. R. Valentiner on the Master of Frankfurt, C. P. Lefèvre on van Orley, H. E. Van Gelder and W. Stechow on Rembrandt, J. Rosenberg on Barent Fabritius, A. Heppner on Teniers, H. E. Wethey on Bartolome Ordoñez and Diego de Siloe, M. S. Soria on Zurbaran, P. Hofer, J. Lopez-Rey, W. S. Cook and M. S. Soria on Goya, J. Thilis on Manet and Baudelaire, G. Rosenthal on Pierre Lepautre, J. Rewald on Renoir, and others. *The Burlington Magazine* 88 (November): 281–83.

"The Wernher Collection." Review of an exhibition at Wildenstein's, London. *The Listener*, October 24: 568.

"An Exhibition of Sienese Art." Review of an exhibition of 13th- to 15th-century Sienese painting and sculpture at the Siena Pinacoteca. *The Burlington Magazine* 88 (March): 71.

"An Exhibition of Sienese Stained Glass." Review of an exhibition of stained glass from churches in Siena and the contado, held at the Siena Pinacoteca. *The Burlington Magazine* 88 (December): 306.

A Sienese Codex of the Divine Comedy. Oxford and London: Phaidon Press Ltd. 35 pages, frontispiece, 15 figures, 82 plates.

Sienese Quattrocento Painting. Oxford and London: Phaidon Press Ltd. 33 pages, 20 figures, 93 plates. French edition: *La peinture siennoise du Quattrocento*. Translation by E. Combe. Paris: Phaidon. 33 pages, 20 figures, 93 plates. German edition: *Quattrocento Malerei in Siena*. London: Phaidon Press Ltd. 34 pages, 20 figures, 93 plates.

"A Relief by Veyrier at Stowe." *The Burlington Magazine* 89 (May): 135.

"A Statue by Veyrier." *The Burlington Magazine* 89 (January): 22.

"*Giovanni di Paolo* by Cesare Brandi." *The Burlington Magazine* 89 (May): 138–39.

"*Goro di Gregorio* by Enzo Carli." *The Burlington Magazine* 89 (July): 200–201.

"*Luca Carlevarijs* by Fabio Mauroner." *The Burlington Magazine* 89 (April): 110.

"The Ghent Altarpiece." Review of *Van Eyck: The Holy Lamb* by Leo van Puyvelde. *The Spectator*, December 26: 805–6.

"Recent Research." Review of periodical articles by M. Meiss on Italian primitives at Konopiste, R. Longhi on the 1945 Venice exhibition, A. Morassi on Titian, O. Brendel on Titian, E. Tietze-Conrat on Tintoretto and Titian, B. Beinert on Titian, W. Suida on Mantegna, A. Morassi on Antonello, C. Baroni on mannerist painting at Cremona, G. Bianchi-Bandinelli on Francesco Vanni, and others. *The Burlington Magazine* 89 (February): 50–52.

"Recent Research." Review of periodical articles by F. J. Mather on Masaccio, G. Ring on Rogier van der Weyden and Memling, J. Bier on Riemenschneider, E. Greindl on Rubens, W. R. Valentiner on Rubens, L. Ozzola on Rubens, H. S. Francis on Rubens, L. R. Lind on Rubens, O. Benesch on Van Dyck, R. McLanathan on Poussin, P. Jamot on Poussin, A. Morassi on El Greco, J. Lopez-Rey on Velázquez, D. Angulo Iniquez on Velázquez, F. J. Sanchez-Canton on Goya, F. S. Wight on Goya, and others. *The Burlington Magazine* 89 (June): 165–67.

"Recent Research." Review of periodical articles by E. Garrison on Berlinghieresque frescoes, G. Coor-Achenbach on Coppo de Marcovaldo and Salerno di Coppo, E. Garrison on Pacino di Buonaguida, R. Offner on Jacopo di Cione, J. Balogh on Italian sculpture at Budapest, C. Seymour and H. Swarzenski on Quercia, R. Krautheimer on 'Maestro Gusmin,' G. Coor-Achenbach on the iconography of Tobias, W. Stechow on Marco del Buono and Apollonio di Giovanni, A. Morassi on Caravaggio, G. Bargelles and E. Arslan on Ercole de' Roberti, B. C. Heyl on Bernardo Strozzi, E. Panofsky on the iconography of Hylas, W. E. Suida on Sebastiano del Piombo, and others. *The Burlington Magazine* 89 (October): 288–91.

"Elizabethan Psychologist: Nicholas Hilliard's Quadricentennial." Review of an exhibition at the Victoria and Albert Museum, London. *Art News* 46 (July): 18–20, 37.

"An Exhibition of Pisan Sculpture." Review of the Mostra della scultura pisana del Trecento at Pisa. *The Listener*, October 6: 680–81.

"Giovanni di Paolo." Letter in response to one from Cesare Brandi. *The Burlington Magazine* 89 (July): 196.

1948

The Drawings of Domenichino in the Collection of His Majesty the King at Windsor Castle. London: Phaidon Press Ltd. 187 pages, 73 figures, 69 plates.

"A Diptych by Francesco di Vannuccio." *The Burlington Magazine* 90 (May): 137–41.

"Florentine Paintings as Social Documents." Review of *Florentine Painting and Its Social Background* by Frederick Antal. *The Listener*, April 15: 632.

"Raphael Germanised." Review of *Raphael* by Oskar Fischel. *The Spectator*, September 17: 376.

"Art and Forgery." Review of *Fakes* by Otto Kurz. *The Spectator*, June 4: 682, 684.

"*Proporzioni* II." Review of the second volume of the periodical *Proporzioni: Studi di storia dell'arte* edited by Roberto Longhi. *The Burlington Magazine* 90 (December): 359–60.

"Master of Northern Baroque." Review of *The Sketches of Rubens* by Leo van Puyvelde. *The Spectator*, March 5: 292, 294.

"Influence from the South." Review of *British Art and the Mediterranean* by Fritz Saxl and Rudolf Wittkower. *The Spectator*, April 23: 498.

"The Advantages of Scholarship." Review of *Rogier van der Weyden* by Walter Ueberwasser, *The Flemish Primitives* by Leo van Puyvelde, *The Master of Mary of Burgundy* by Otto Paecht, and *Studies in Seicento Art and Theory* by Denis Mahon. *The Spectator*, November 19: 670.

"Recent Research." Review of periodical articles by E. Tolaini and G. Swarzenski on Arnolfo di Cambio, W. R. Valentiner on Giovanni di Balduccio and Andrea Pisano, G. Mariacher on Nino Pisano, R. Longhi on Venetian painting, H. Tietze on Giovanni Bellini, G. Fiocco on Pietro dei Marescalchi, W. Arslan on Domenico Brusasorci, E. Tietze-Conrat on Pasquale Ottini, J. Hess on Raphael and Guilio Romano, E. P. Richardson on Annibale Caracci, and W. S. Heckscher on Bernini. *The Burlington Magazine* 90 (June): 177–78.

1949

Donatello's Relief of the Ascension with Christ Giving the Keys to St. Peter. Victoria and Albert Museum Monograph no. 1. London: His Majesty's Stationery Office. 12 pages, folding frontispiece, 5 figures, 12 plates.

A Lecture on Nicholas Hilliard. London: Home and Van Thal Ltd. 29 pages, frontispiece, 32 plates.

The Virgin with the Laughing Child. Victoria and Albert Museum Monograph no. 2. London: His Majesty's Stationery Office. 10 pages, frontispiece, 10 figures, 12 plates.

"Notes on a Florentine Tomb Front." *The Burlington Magazine* 91 (April): 94–97.

"Three Panels by Simone Martini." *The Burlington Magazine* 91 (July): 195–96.

"Florentine Confusion." Review of *The Florentine Portrait* by Jean Alazard. *The Spectator*, February 11: 196, 198.

"Art and Nature." Review of *Landscape into Art* by Kenneth Clark. *The Observer*, November 27: 7.

"*Nicola, Arnolfo, Lapo: L'Arca di S. Domenico in Bologna* by Cesare Gnudi." *The Burlington Magazine* 91 (December): 358–59.

"Quattrocento Sculptor." Review of *Ghiberti* by Ludwig Goldscheider. *The Times Literary Supplement*, December 9: 806.

"Iconography of a Saint." Review of *St. Catherine in Tuscan Painting* by George Kaftal. *The Times Literary Supplement*, July 1: 426.

"Apology for Painting." Review of *Paragone: A Comparison of the Arts by Leonardo da Vinci*, with an introduction and translation by Irma A. Richter. *The Times Literary Supplement*, June 10: 376.

"Tintoretto." Review of *Tintoretto* by Hans Tietze. *The Observer*, June 12: 6.

"Recent Research." Review of periodical articles by A. de Capitani d'Arzago on frescoes at Castelseprio, L. Zovatto on frescoes at Concordia, E. Carli on Giovanni di Agostino, C. Brandi on Pietro Lorenzetti, W. E. Suida on Lippo Vanni, L. Becherucci on Orcagna, L. Coletti on Pisanello, R. G. Mather on 15th-century Florentine *Portate al Catasto*, R. Krautheimer on architectural panels at Baltimore and Urbino, P. Toesca on Marmitta, W. E. Suida on a marble bust of Simonetta Vespucci ascribed to Leonardo, F. Antal on Girolamo da Carpi, E. Tietze-Conrat on Dosso Dossi, A. Mezzetti on Antonio Gherardi, E. D. Barton on Bernini, and others. *The Burlington Magazine* 91 (January): 23–25.

"Recent Research." Review of periodical articles by S. Ortolani on 12th-century South Italian Romanesque frescoes, T. Rousseau on Castagno, G. Poggi on Ghiberti, L. Planiscig on Donatello, E. P. Richardson on Desiderio, P. Meller on Giovanni Dalmata, W. Heil on Verrocchio, W. M. Milliken on Riccio, C. Gilbert on Michelangelo, H. Tietze and E. Tietze-Conrat on the Allendale Nativity, L. Burroughs on Parmigianino, H. B. Wehle on Tintoretto, R. Bonelli on Ippolito Scalza, and others. *The Burlington Magazine* 91 (August): 233–34.

"Drawings from Chatsworth." Review of an exhibition of 72 drawings from the collection of the Duke of Devonshire organized by the Arts Council, London. *The Listener*, April 21: 665–66.

"Masterpieces from the Pinakothek." Review of an exhibition of paintings from Munich held at the National Gallery, London. *The Listener*, May 5: 747.

"Paintings from Vienna." Review of an exhibition of paintings from the Kunsthistorisches Museum held at the Tate Gallery, London. *The Listener*, May 26: 831.

"Works of Art from Vienna." A second review of the Kunsthistorisches Museum exhibition at the Tate Gallery, London. *The Listener,* June 2: 942.

"An Exhibition of Sienese Wooden Sculpture." Review of the Mostra della antica scultura lignea senese held at the Palazzo Pubblico, Siena. *The Burlington Magazine* 91 (November): 323–24.

Introduction and notes to *The Life of Benvenuto Cellini Written by Himself* translated by John Addington Symonds. London: Phaidon Press Ltd. 498 pages, 57 illustrations.

1950

The Complete Work of Paolo Uccello. London: Phaidon Press Ltd. 1–31, 141–73 pages, color frontispiece, 61 figures, 1 folding color plate, 1 unnumbered color plate, 2 folding black-and-white plates, 108 plates.

The Raphael Cartoons. Victoria and Albert Museum Large Picture Book no. 5. London: His Majesty's Stationery Office. 10 pages, 30 plates.

"A Cartapesta Mirror Frame." *The Burlington Magazine* 92 (October): 288–91.

"Matteo di Giovanni's Assumption Altarpiece." *Proporzioni* 3: 81–85.

"The Enchantment of Life." Review of *Aesthetics and History* by Bernard Berenson. *The Times Literary Supplement,* April 7: 209–10.

"*Landscape, Portrait, Still-Life: Their Origin and Development* by Max J. Friedländer." *The Listener,* January 5: 35–36.

"The Personality of Holbein." Review of *Holbein: The Complete Paintings* by Paul Ganz. *The Listener,* July 20: 100.

"The van Beuningen Pictures." Review of the *Catalogue of the D. G. van Beuningen Collection* by Dr. D. Hannema. *The Times Literary Supplement,* May 12: 288.

"*Lorenzo Ghiberti* by Leo Planiscig." *The Burlington Magazine* 92 (February): 57.

"French Primitive Painting." Review of *A Century of French Painting, 1400–1500* by Grete Ring. *The Listener,* January 12: 76.

"Recent Research." Review of periodical articles by E. Carli on Nicola Pisano and Jacopo della Quercia, O. Morisani on Tino di Camaino, L. Coletti on Duccio and Simone Martini, G. Paccagnini on Lippo Memmi, G. Vigni on Giovanni di Nicola and Lippo Memmi, H. Friedman on Giovanni Baronzio, W. R. Valentiner on Donatello and Nanni di Banco, W. Milliken on Nanni di Banco, M. Davies on Lorenzo Monaco, M. Salmi on Paolo Uccello and Francesco di Giorgio, P. Sanpaolesi on Francesco di Giorgio, G. Marchini on Giuliano da Sangallo, C. C. Ragghianti on Raffaellino del Garbo and Andrea del Sarto, C. H. Smyth on Bronzino, and others. *The Burlington Magazine* 92 (April): 115–17.

"Recent Research (continued)." Review of periodical articles by G. Fiocco on Venetian painting at Konopiste, R. Longhi on Bassano, E. Rigoni on Niccolò Pizzolo and Donatello, G. Mariacher on Antonio Rizzo, H. Tietze on Venetian 16-century drawings and on Titian, W. Suida on Moroni, M. de Benedetti on Caravaggio, L. Venturi on Caravaggio, J. Ainaud on Caravaggio, M. Lorente on Bernini, R. Wittkower on Bernini. *The Burlington Magazine* 92 (May): 142–43.

"Bolognese Trecento Painting." Review of an exhibition held at Bologna. *The Listener,* September 28: 428.

"An Exhibition of Biccherna Covers." Review of an exhibition held at Florence and Siena. *The Burlington Magazine* 92 (November): 320.

"A Saint of Siena: The 'Mostra Bernardiniana.'" Review of an exhibition at Siena commemorating the fifth centenary of St. Bernardino's canonization. *The Tablet*, September 9: 210.

"A Sodoma Exhibition." Review of an exhibition at Vercelli and Siena commemorating the fourth centenary of Sodoma's death with a catalogue by Professor Carli. *The Burlington Magazine* 92 (November): 326.

Letter in reply to one from Maurice W. Brockwell. *The Times Literary Supplement*, July 7: 421.

1951

"The Arca of St. Dominic: A Hypothesis." *The Burlington Magazine* 93 (November): 347–51.

"The Early Style of Domenico Veneziano." *The Burlington Magazine* 93 (July): 216–23.

"*Quattrocentisti Senesi* by Cesare Brandi." *The Art Bulletin* 33 (June): 141–43.

"Piero della Francesca: The Development of a Visionary." Review of *Piero della Francesca* by Kenneth Clark. *The Times Literary Supplement*, March 23: 172–74.

"Early Italian Art." Review of *National Gallery Catalogues: The Earlier Italian Schools* by Martin Davies. *The Times Literary Supplement*, November 16: 726.

"The Work of Parmigianino." Review of *Parmigianino* by Sydney J. Freedberg. *The Times Literary Supplement*, January 26: 51.

"Roger Fry's Art Criticism." Review of *French, Flemish, and British Art* by Roger Fry. *The Times Literary Supplement*, October 12: 644.

"The Franciscan Legend." Review of *St. Francis in Italian Painting* by George Kaftal. *The Times Literary Supplement*, January 12: 16.

"*Masterpieces of Sculpture from the National Gallery of Art* by Charles Seymour, Jr." *The Burlington Magazine* 93 (March): 98.

"The Study of Titian." Review of *Titian: Paintings and Drawings* by Hans Tietze. *The Spectator*, January 5: 22.

"Speculations on Sculpture." Review of *Studies of Italian Renaissance Sculpture* by W. R. Valentiner. *The Times Literary Supplement*, February 23: 112.

"Recent Research." Review of periodical articles by C. Brandi on Coppo di Marcovaldo, G. Swarzenski on 14th-century biccherna covers, G. Brunetti on Agostino di Duccio, O. Sirén on Francesco di Simone, R. Longhi on Masaccio, M. Salmi on Fra Angelico, L. Ragghianti on Domenico di Michelino, M. Davies on Fra Filippo Lippi, F. Zeri on Girolamo da Cremona, A. M. Brizio, G. Fiocco, H. Tietze and E. Tietze-Conrat, R. Gallo, B. Degenhart, and W. E. Suida on Bellini, R. L. Douglas on Giorgione, R. Pallucchini on Giorgione, A. M. Romanini on Albertino and Martino Piazza, F. Hartt on Raphael and Michelangelo, and others. *The Burlington Magazine* 93 (February): 62–64.

"Recent Research (continued)." Review of periodical articles by R. Longhi on Caravaggesque paintings and Serodine, V. Martinelli on Bernini and Pietro da Cortona's tapestry cartoons, G. Briganti on Giovanni da San Giovanni, and R. Wittkower on drawings by Juvarra. *The Burlington Magazine* 93 (March): 95.

"The Arezzo Exhibition." Review of the Mostra d'arte sacra at Arezzo. *The Burlington Magazine* 93 (January): 26–27.

"Sir Thomas Lawrence." Review of an exhibition at Agnew's, London. *The Listener*, June 7: 926.

Fra Angelico. London: Phaidon Press Ltd. 1–31, 165–213 pages, color frontispiece, 65 figures, 6 color plates, 133 black-and-white plates.

Italian Gothic Sculpture in the Victoria and Albert Museum. Victoria and Albert Museum Monograph no. 5. London: Her Majesty's Stationery Office. 30 pages, 21 figures, 32 plates.

The Virgin and Child by Agostino di Duccio. Victoria and Albert Museum Monograph no. 6. London: His Majesty's Stationery Office. 16 pages, frontispiece, 11 figures, 10 plates.

"A Caricature by Domenichino." *The Burlington Magazine* 94 (June): 167–68.

"A Statuette by Antonio Minelli." *The Burlington Magazine* 94 (January): 24–28.

"The Earliest Modern Painters?" Review of *Van Eyck* by Ludwig Baldass. *The Listener*, May 1: 720.

"Medallic Likenesses." Review of *Unknown Renaissance Portraits: Medals of Famous Men and Women of the XV and XVI Centuries* by Ludwig Goldscheider. *The Times Literary Supplement*, June 13: 392.

"*Michelangelo Drawings* edited by Ludwig Goldscheider." *The Listener*, January 3: 32.

"The Art of Vermeer." Review of *Vermeer* by Lawrence Gowing. *The Times Literary Supplement*, September 19: 608.

"Florentine Painting in the Late Trecento." Review of *Painting in Florence and Siena after the Black Death* by Millard Meiss. *The Times Literary Supplement*, May 23: 340.

"A Re-examination of Tintoretto." Review of *Tintoretto* by Eric Newton. *The Times Literary Supplement*, February 8: 104.

"*La Pinacoteca di Cremona* by Alfredo Puerari." *The Burlington Magazine* 94 (May): 152.

"Leonardo's Notebooks." Review of *Selections from the Notebooks of Leonardo da Vinci* by Irma A. Richter. *The Times Literary Supplement*, October 3: 640.

"A Century of Italian Art." Review of *Il Trecento* by Pietro Toesca. *The Times Literary Supplement*, October 31: 704.

"*Nanni* by Paolo Vaccarino." *The Burlington Magazine* 94 (June): 182.

"*Gothic and Renaissance Sculptures in the Collection of the Los Angeles County Museum: Catalogue and Guide* by W. R. Valentiner." *The Burlington Magazine* 94 (February): 61.

"Carracci Drawings in the Royal Collection." Review of *The Drawings of the Carracci in the Collection of Her Majesty the Queen at Windsor Castle* by Rudolf Wittkower. *The Times Literary Supplement*, December 26: 848.

"Art and Style." Review of *Classic Art: An Introduction to the Italian Renaissance* by Heinrich Wölfflin. *The Times Literary Supplement*, December 19: 828–29.

"Thinker and Artist." Review of *Leonardo da Vinci: An Account of His Development as an Artist* by Kenneth Clark and *Leonardo da Vinci: Landscapes and Plants* edited by Ludwig Goldscheider. *The Times Literary Supplement*, July 11: 448.

"Recent Research." Review of periodical articles by A. Grabar on the Castelseprio frescoes, E. Garrison on 13th-century Sienese paintings and on Berlinghiero and Deodato Orlandi, G. Coor on Coppo di Marcovaldo, E. Carli on Guido da Siena, M. Meiss on Duccio, R. Longhi on Stefano Fiorentino, L. Coletti on the Maestro colorista di Assisi, M. Eisenberg on Mariotto di Nardo, C. Volpe and F. Zeri on Ambrogio Lorenzetti, R. Pallucchini on Paolo Veneziano, P. Bettini on Arnolfo di Cambio, W. R. Valentiner on Ramo di Paganello, G. Swarzenski on 15th-century sculpture, L. Grassi on Gentile da Fabriano, B. Degenhart on Pisanello, M. Salmi on Fra Angelico, L. Collobi-Ragghianti on Zanobi Stozzi, B. Bearzi on Donatello, and others. *The Burlington Magazine* 94 (March): 82–87.

"Dutch Art." Review of an exhibition held at Burlington House, London. *The Listener*, December 11: 992.

"The Leonardo da Vinci Exhibition." Review of an exhibition organized by the Royal Academy of Arts, London, to celebrate the 500th anniversary of Leonardo's birth. *The Listener*, March 20: 484.

"The Sta. Maria Maggiore Altarpiece." Letter concerning Kenneth Clark's reconstruction of Masaccio's Roman altarpiece. *The Burlington Magazine* 94 (January): 31–32.

1953

"Elizabethan Style." *Art News* 52 (June-July-August): 40–49, 73.

"Some Bronze Statuettes by Francesco Fanelli." *The Burlington Magazine* 95 (May): 157–62.

"The Barber Institute." Review of the *Catalogue of the Paintings, Drawings and Miniatures in the Barber Institute of Fine Arts, University of Birmingham. The Times Literary Supplement,* January 2: 4.

"B. B.: Interpreter of the Renaissance." Review of *The Italian Painters of the Renaissance* by Bernard Berenson. *The Times Literary Supplement*, August 28: vi.

"Problem Picture." Review of *The Pseudo-Arnolfini Portrait: A Case of Mistaken Identity* by Maurice W. Brockwell. *The Times Literary Supplement,* January 9: 20.

"Antelami's Achievements." Review of *Benedetto Antelami: Architetto e scultore e l'arte del suo tempo* by Géza de Francovich. *The Times Literary Supplement,* July 24: 472.

"Michelangelo's Arts." Review of *Michelangelo: Paintings, Sculptures, Architecture* by Ludwig Goldscheider. *The Times Literary Supplement*, October 9: 640.

"Franciscan Pilgrimage." Review of *Assisi and Umbria Revisited* by Edward Hutton. *The Times Literary Supplement*, December 18: 820.

"Saints and Their Legends in Art." Review of *Iconography of the Saints in Tuscan Painting* by George Kaftal. *The Times Literary Supplement*, January 23: 52.

"Rembrandt's Etchings." Review of *Rembrandt's Etchings* by Ludwig Münz. *The Listener*, January 8: 69.

"A New History of Art." Review of *Painting in Britain, 1530–1790* by E. K. Waterhouse. *The Spectator*, June 12: 764, 766.

"The Flemish Primitives." Review of *Les primitifs flamands. I. Corpus de la peinture des anciens Pays-Bas méridionaux au 15e siècle.* Volume 1, *Le Musée communal de Bruges* by Aquilin Janssens de Bisthoven and R. A. Parmentier. Volume 2, *La Galerie Sabauda de Turin* by Carlo Aru and Et. de Geradon. *The Times Literary Supplement*, December 11: 803.

"Recent Research." Review of periodical articles by O. Morisani and S. Bottari on the tomb of Frederick II, W. R. Valentiner on Nicola Pisano and Donatello, G. Brunetti on Tino da Camaino, D. Frey on Giotto, G. Coor-Achenbach on the Master of the Badia ad Isola, R. Krautheimer on the Fonte Gaia at Siena, G. Brunetti on Jacopo della Quercia, E. P. Richardson on Ghiberti, G. Fiocco on Michele da Firenze, G. Marchini on Maso di Bartolommeo and Donatello's workshop, M. Salmi on Brunelleschi, Masaccio and Masolino, R. Longhi on the Pratovecchio Master, G. Paccagnini on Domenico Veneziano, L. H. Heydenreich on Jacopo del Sellaio, and others. *The Burlington Magazine* 95 (August): 277–81.

"Flemish Painting." Review of an exhibition at Burlington House, London. *The Listener*, December 10: 1010.

"Lorenzo Lotto." Review of an exhibition at Venice. *The Listener,* September 17: 472.

"Signorelli and Luini." Review of the exhibitions of Luca Signorelli at Cortona and Bernardino Luini at Como. *The Listener,* November 5: 778.

"Art and Style." Reply to a letter from Herbert Read about Peter and Linda Murray's translation of Heinrich Wölfflin's *Die klassische Kunst. The Times Literary Supplement,* January 2: 9.

"The Bust of Mr. Baker." Letter concerning an article by Rudolf Wittkower on Bernini's portrait of Thomas Baker. *The Burlington Magazine* 95 (April): 138–39.

1954

The Metropolitan Museum of Art Miniatures: Piero della Francesca, about 1420–1492. New York: Book-of-the-Month Club, Inc. 25 unnumbered pages, 24 color "miniatures."

Samson and a Philistine by Giovanni Bologna. Victoria and Albert Museum Monograph no. 8. London: Her Majesty's Stationery Office. 20 pages, 14 figures, 14 plates.

"Two Paduan Bronzes." *The Burlington Magazine* 96 (January): 9–13.

"Tudor Portraits." Review of *Tudor Artists* by Erna Auerbach. *The Tablet,* July 10: 36.

"The Drawings of G. B. Castiglione and Stefano della Bella in the Royal Library at Windsor Castle by Anthony Blunt." *The Listener,* October 14: 637.

"Italian Renaissance Art." Review of *England and the Italian Renaissance: The Growth of Interest in Its History and Art* by J. R. Hale. *The Times Literary Supplement,* June 18: 392.

"Essays for Belle da Costa Greene." Review of *Studies in Art and*

Literature for Belle da Costa Greene edited by Dorothy Miner. *The Times Literary Supplement*, October 29: 690.

"Flemish Master Painters." Review of *Early Netherlandish Painting: Its Origins and Character* by Erwin Panofsky. *The Times Literary Supplement*, March 5: 156.

"Venetian Painter." Review of *Vincenzo Catena* by Giles Robertson. *The Times Literary Supplement*, October 8: 636.

"The Christ Child in Italian Art." Review of *The Christ Child in Devotional Images in Italy during the XIV Century* by Dorothy C. Shorr. *The Times Literary Supplement*, June 4: 356.

"The Figurative Arts." Reviews of *Piero della Francesca* and *The Arch of Constantine* by Bernard Berenson. *The Times Literary Supplement*, October 15: 652.

"Flemish Primitives." Review of *Les primitifs flamands. I. Corpus de la peinture des anciens Pays-Bas méridionaux au 15e siècle*. Volume 3, *The National Gallery, London* by Martin Davies, and *Les primitifs flamands. II. Répertoire des peintures flamandes des 15e et 16e siècles*. Volume 1, *Collections d'Espagne* by Jacques Lavalleye. *The Times Literary Supplement*, September 24: 604.

"Judgment upon Caravaggio." Review of *Michelangelo Merisi da Caravaggio* and *Caravaggio's Death of the Virgin* by Roger Hinks, and *Caravaggio: His Incongruity and His Fame* by Bernard Berenson. *The Times Literary Supplement*, January 15: 40.

"Rubens Sketches at Rotterdam." Review of an exhibition at the Boymans Museum, Rotterdam. *The Listener*, February 11: 266.

1955

An Introduction to Italian Sculpture. Part 1. *Italian Gothic Sculpture*. London: Phaidon Press Ltd. 2–62, 176–224, 22 unnumbered pages, 101 figures, 108 plates.

"The Essence of Caravaggio's Art." Review of *Caravaggio Studies* by Walter Friedlaender. *The Times Literary Supplement*, July 29: 424.

"London Art Treasures." Review of *The National Gallery, London* by Philip Hendy. *The Times Literary Supplement*, November 18: 684.

"Great Painting." Review of *The Fifteenth Century from van Eyck to Botticelli* by Jacques Lassaigne and Giulio Carlo Argan. *The Times Literary Supplement*, November 25: 708.

"Italian Engraving of the 15th Century." Review of *Early Florentine Designers and Engravers* by John Goldsmith Phillips. *The Times Literary Supplement*, December 2: 727.

"The Bruges Madonna." Review of *La Madonna di Bruges di Michelangiolo* by Giovanni Poggi. *The Times Literary Supplement*, August 5: 440.

"Bramante and Bramantino." Review of *Bramante Pittore e il Bramantino* by William Suida. *The Times Literary Supplement*, May 20: 264.

"Andrea Mantegna." Review of *Mantegna* by Erica Tietze-Conrat. *The Times Literary Supplement*, June 24: 346.

"Gian Lorenzo Bernini." Review of *Gian Lorenzo Bernini: The Sculptor of the Roman Baroque* by Rudolph Wittkower. *The Times Literary Supplement*, December 23: 769–70.

1956

" 'Michelangelo's Cupid:' The End of a Chapter." *The Burlington Magazine* 98 (November): 403–11.

"Rethinking Sassetta." *The Burlington Magazine* 98 (October): 364–70.

"Introduction to the Flemish Painters." Review of *Early Netherlandish Painting: From van Eyck to Bruegel* by Max J. Friedländer. *The Times Literary Supplement*, October 26: 628.

"Florentine Church Treasures." Review of *Die Kirchen von Florenz* by Walter and Elisabeth Paatz. *The Times Literary Supplement*, February 10: 80.

"Italian Master Drawings at Oxford." Review of the *Catalogue of the Collection of Drawings in the Ashmolean Museum*. Volume 2, *Italian Schools* by K. T. Parker. *The Times Literary Supplement*, November 2: 644.

"Dr. W. L. Hildburgh." Obituary. *The Burlington Magazine* 98 (February): 56.

1957

The Virgin with the Laughing Child. Reprint of the 1949 edition. Victoria and Albert Museum Monograph no. 2. London: His Majesty's Stationery Office. 10 pages, frontispiece, 10 figures, 12 plates.

"Italian Art in the Louvre." Review of *Louvre: Masterpieces of Italian Painting* by Germain Bazin. *The Times Literary Supplement*, January 4: 4.

"Artists of the Renaissance." Review of *An Introduction to Italian Renaissance Painting* by Cecil Gould. *The Times Literary Supplement*, May 31: 332.

"Sculptor of the Italian Renaissance." Review of *Lorenzo Ghiberti* by Richard Krautheimer in collaboration with Trude Krautheimer-Hess. *The Times Literary Supplement*, April 26: 254.

"A Leonardo Symposium." Review of the English edition of *Leonardo da Vinci*, a collection of essays by various hands first published in 1939 to accompany the exhibition at Milan, Mostra di Leonardo da Vinci e delle invenzioni italiane. *The Times Literary Supplement*, December 13: 752.

"Painters of Ferrara." Review of the revised edition of *Officina ferrarese* by Roberto Longhi. *The Times Literary Supplement,* February 1: 60.

"Miniatures by Mantegna?" Review of *Andrea Mantegna as Illuminator* by Millard Meiss. *The Times Literary Supplement,* July 26: 452.

"Artist of the Sienese School." Review of *Simone Martini* by Giovanni Paccagnini. *The Times Literary Supplement,* December 20: 768.

"The Space Illusion in the Quattrocento." Review of *The Birth and Rebirth of Pictorial Space* by John White. *The Times Literary Supplement,* October 18: 620.

"Workers in Bronze." Review of *Bayerisches Nationalmuseum, München. Katalog XIII, 5, Die Bildwerke in Bronze und in anderen Metallen* by Hans R. Weihrauch. *The Times Literary Supplement,* January 4: 4.

"Italian and Flemish." Review of *Antonello da Messina* by Stefano Bottari, *Italian Painting: Twelve Centuries of Art in Italy* by Edith Appleton Standen, and *Flemish Painting: The Century of van Eyck* by Jacques Lassaigne. *The Times Literary Supplement,* December 27: 784.

"Italian Masters." Review of *Mosaici di Ravenna* by Giuseppe Bovini, *Masaccio: Frescoes in Florence* by Sir Philip Hendy, *Italian Miniatures* by Mario Salmi, and *Francesco Guardi* by Vittorio Moschini. *The Times Literary Supplement,* May 3: 268.

"Church Art." Review of *San Vitale, Ravenna* by Giuseppe Bovini and *Fra Angelico, 1387–1455* by Paolo d'Ancona. *The Times Literary Supplement,* June 28: 392.

1958

An Introduction to Italian Sculpture. Part 2. *Italian Renaissance Sculpture.* London: Phaidon Press Ltd. 2–117, 268–363, 20 unnumbered pages, 165 figures, 144 plates.

The Raphael Cartoons. Reprint of the 1950 edition. Victoria and Albert Museum Large Picture Book no. 5. London: Her Majesty's Stationery Office. 10 pages, 30 plates.

"Andrea da Pontedera." In *Enciclopedia universale dell'arte.* Volume 1: 383–87. Venice and Rome: Istituto per la Collaborazione Culturale.

"Giovanni Pisano." In *Enciclopedia universale dell'arte.* Volume 6: 239–46. Venice and Rome: Istituto per la Collaborazione Culturale.

"Sassetta and Giovanni di Paolo: The Mystic and the Fantastic in Renaissance Siena." *Art News Annual* 27: 125–54, 179–81.

"Cajoling Connoisseur." Review of *Essays in Appreciation* by Bernard Berenson. *The Times Literary Supplement,* May 9: 252.

"Attraction of Brueghel." Review of *Peter Brueghel the Elder* by Gustav Glück. *The Times Literary Supplement,* June 20: 343.

"Problematical Ferrarese Painter." Review of *Cosimo Tura* by Eberhard Ruhmer. *The Times Literary Supplement,* April 11: 192.

"Italian Masterpieces." Review of *Sienese Painting* by Enzo Carli, *Mantegna: La Cappella Ovetari nella Chiesa degli Eremitani* by Giuseppe Fiocco, *Affreschi di Masolino a Castiglione Olona* by Pietro Toesca, and *I Vivarini* by Vittorio Moschini. *The Times Literary Supplement,* June 27: 356.

"Flemish and Italian Masters." Review of *Flemish Painting: From Bosch to Rubens* by Jacques Lassaigne and Robert L. Delevoy, *Louvre: Masterpieces of Italian Painting* by Germain Bazin, and *Venetian Painting* by Jean-Louis Vaudoyer. *The Times Literary Supplement,* November 28: 692.

1959

"Andrea da Pontedera." In *Encyclopedia of World Art.* Volume 1: 420–24. New York, Toronto, and London: McGraw Hill Book

Company, Inc. Originally published in Italian in *Enciclopedia universale dell'arte*, 1958.

"The Martelli David." *The Burlington Magazine* 101 (April): 134–39.

"A Relief by Sansovino." *The Burlington Magazine* 101 (January): 4–10.

"A Small Bronze by Tribolo." *The Burlington Magazine* 101 (March): 85–89.

"Some Donatello Problems." In *Studies in the History of Art Dedicated to William E. Suida on His Eightieth Birthday*: 47–65. London: Phaidon Press Ltd.

"A Botticelli Album." Review of *Botticelli* by André Chastel. *The Times Literary Supplement*, June 5: 332.

"Venetian High Renaissance." Review of *National Gallery Catalogues: The Sixteenth-Century Venetian School* by Cecil Gould. *The Times Literary Supplement*, February 6: 68.

"Illusionist Painter." Review of *Giulio Romano* by Frederick Hartt. *The Times Literary Supplement*, August 28: 492.

"Feeling One's Way in Florence." Review of *The Stones of Florence* by Mary McCarthy. *The Times Literary Supplement*, November 13: 662.

"The Image of Our Lord on Earth." Review of *The Life of Christ* by John Rothenstein. *The Times Literary Supplement*, December 4: 704.

"From a Sienese Workshop." Review of *Ambrogio Lorenzetti* by George Rowley. *The Times Literary Supplement*, March 27: 172.

"Privately Collected." Review of *Italian Paintings and Drawings at 56 Princes Gate, London, S.W.7* [by Antoine Seilern]. *The Times Literary Supplement*, July 3: 396.

"Honouring an Art Historian." Review of *Studies in the History of Art Dedicated to William E. Suida on His Eightieth Birthday*. *The Times Literary Supplement*, October 30: 620.

"The Dutch Scene." Review of *A History of Dutch Life and Art* by J. J. M. Timmers. *The Times Literary Supplement*, October 2: 563.

"Venetian Mosaic Art." Review of *The Mosaics in the Church of St. Mark in Venice* by Pietro Toesca and Ferdinando Forlati. *The Times Literary Supplement*, April 10: 207.

"A Selective Tour of the Italian Arts." Review of *Art and Architecture in Italy, 1600–1750* by Rudolf Wittkower. *The Times Literary Supplement*, January 30: 61.

"A Great Also-Ran." Review of *Jacopo Bassano* by Pietro Zampetti. *The Times Literary Supplement*, January 23: 49.

"Language of Art." Review of *Giotto and His Contemporaries* by Enzo Carli, and *Twenty Centuries of Great European Painting* by Hiltgart Keller and Bodo Cichy. *The Times Literary Supplement*, February 27: 116.

"Florentine Art." Review of *Studies in the Florentine Churches*. Part 1, *Pre-Renaissance Period* by Evelyn Sandberg-Vavalà, and *An Index of Attributions made in Tuscan Sources before Vasari* by Peter Murray. *The Times Literary Supplement*, August 7: 456.

"The Two 'St Georges.' " Letter to the editor correcting Sylvia Sprigge's misstatements about the author's opinion of the National Gallery's newly acquired painting by Uccello. *The Manchester Guardian*, January 28: 6.

1960

"A Crucifixion by Matteo di Giovanni." *The Burlington Magazine* 102 (February): 63–67.

"The Fresco in Its Setting." Review of *The Mural Painters of Tuscany* by Eve Borsook. *The Times Literary Supplement*, June 17: 382.

"The Art of Fresco." Review of *Giotto* by Cesare Gnudi. *The Times Literary Supplement*, December 9: 792.

"Questions of Style." Review of *National Gallery Catalogues: The Dutch School* by Neil MacLaren. *The Times Literary Supplement*, June 24: 396.

"Looking Again." Review of *Giotto and Assisi* by Millard Meiss. *The Times Literary Supplement*, August 5: 492.

"The Dutch School." Review of *National Gallery Catalogues, Dutch School, XVII–XIX Centuries: Plates. The Times Literary Supplement*, June 24: 396.

"The Line of Life." Review of *Great Draughtsmen from Pisanello to Picasso* by Jakob Rosenberg. *The Times Literary Supplement*, February 26: 124.

"Circumscribed Private View." Review of *Flemish Painters* by R. H. Wilenski. *The Times Literary Supplement*, June 3: 348.

"Measure of the Masters." Review of *Giotto* by Eugenio Battisti, *Velázquez* by Enrique Lafluente Ferrari, *Pietro Cavallini* by Pietro Toesca, *Paolo Uccello* by Paolo D'Ancona and *Utrillo* by Waldemar George. *The Times Literary Supplement*, August 26: 540.

"Italian Paintings." Review of *Giovanni Bellini* by Giuseppe Fiocco, *Giotto* by Emilio Cecchi, *Botticelli and His Contemporaries* by Angela Ottino della Chiesa, and *Canaletto and His Contemporaries* by Decio Gioseffi. *The Times Literary Supplement*, December 23: 827.

"Flemish Pictures in Spain." Review of *Les primitifs flamands. II. Répertoire des peintures flamands des 15e et 16e siècles*. Volume 2, *Collections d'Espagne* by Jacques Lavalleye, and *Les primitifs flamands. I. Corpus de la peinture des anciens Pays-Bas méridionaux au 15e siècle*. Volume 1, *Musée Communal des Beaux-Arts, Bruges* by Aquilin Janssens de Bisthoven. *The Times Literary Supplement*, February 19: 108.

"First Lives of the Artists." Review of *Lives of the Most Eminent Painters, Sculptors, and Architects by Giorgio Vasari* edited by Robert N. Linscott, and *Vasari's Lives of the Artists* edited by Betty Burroughs. *The Times Literary Supplement*, September 30: 624.

"Portrait of an Art Historian." Review of *Berenson* by Sylvia Sprigge, *The Passionate Sightseer* and *One Year's Reading for Fun* by Bernard Berenson. *The Times Literary Supplement*, March 25: 185–87.

1961

"Two Paduan Chimney-Pieces." *Arte antica e moderna* nos. 13–16: 151–53.

"Italian Drawings at Windsor." Review of *The Roman Drawings of the XVIIth and XVIIIth Centuries in the Collection of Her Majesty The Queen at Windsor Castle* by Anthony Blunt and H. L. Cooke. *The Times Literary Supplement*, February 17: 100.

"Pen Portrait." Review of *The Life of Michelangelo* by Charles H. Morgan. *The Times Literary Supplement*, March 3: 134.

"Master of Connoisseurship." Review of *Italienische Malerei der Renaissance im Briefwechsel von Giovanni Morelli und Jeanne-Paul Richter, 1876–1891* edited by Irma and Gisela Richter. *The Times Literary Supplement*, May 26: 320.

Introduction and entries for loans from non-Italian sources in the exhibition catalogue *Italian Bronze Statuettes*. London: The Arts Council. 47 unnumbered pages, 32 plates.

Introduction and extensive revisions of many entries in the exhibition catalogue *Meersters van het brons der Italiaanse Renaissance*. Amsterdam: Rijksmuseum. 94 unnumbered pages, 94 illustrations.

1962

Heptatych: Ugolino da Siena. Williamstown, Massachusetts: Sterling and Francine Clark Art Institute. 15 pages, 14 plates (1 color).

"Giovanni di Paolo." In *Encyclopedia of World Art*. Volume 6: 357. New York, Toronto, and London: McGraw Hill Book Company, Inc.

"Giovanni Pisano." In *Encyclopedia of World Art*. Volume 6: 358–65. New York, Toronto, and London: McGraw Hill Book Company, Inc. Originally published in Italian in 1958.

"Renaissance Prologue for Williamstown, Mass." *Art News* 61 (September): 42–43, 50, 52. Abridged from the Clark Art Institute booklet *Heptatych: Ugolino da Siena*.

"Papal Splendour." Review of *Treasures of the Vatican* by Maurizio Calvesi. *The Times Literary Supplement*, December 28: 1000.

"Fifteenth-Century Aesthete." Review of *Neroccio de' Landi, 1447–1500* by Gertrude Coor. *The Times Literary Supplement*, July 20: 520.

"Masters of Metal." Review of *Bronzes, Other Metalwork, and Sculpture in the Irwin Untermyer Collection* by Yvonne Hackenbroch. *The Times Literary Supplement*, September 7: 668.

"As Fresh and Alert as Ever." Review of *Scritti Giovanili, 1912–1922* by Roberto Longhi. *The Times Literary Supplement*, August 10: 580.

"The Altenburg Panel Paintings." Review of *Frühe italienische Malerei in Altenburg. Beschreibender Katalog der Gemälde des 13. bis 16. Jahrhunderts im Staatlichen Lindenau Museum* by Robert Oertel. *The Times Literary Supplement*, July 13: 504.

"Florentine Frescoes." Review of *The Painting of The Life of St. Francis of Assisi* by Leonetto Tintori and Millard Meiss. *The Times Literary Supplement*, September 14: 684.

"From the Renaissance Climax." Review of *The Architecture of Michelangelo* by James S. Ackerman, *Painting of the High Renaissance* by S. J. Freedberg, and *The Genius of Leonardo da Vinci* by André Chastel. *Art News* 60 (January): 43, 51.

"Reading and Looking." Review of *Le pitture di Mantegna* by Giuseppe Fiocco and *European Painting in the 15th Century* by Renzo Chiarelli, Margherita Lenzini Moriondo, and Franco Mozzini. *The Times Literary Supplement*, May 18: 352.

Introduction and various unsigned entries in the exhibition catalogue *Bronzetti italiani del Rinascimento: Catalogo della mostra in Palazzo Strozzi.* Florence: L. S. Olschki. 194 unnumbered pages, 100 illustrations.

1963

An Introduction to Italian Sculpture. Part 3. *Italian High Renaissance and Baroque Sculpture.* 3 volumes. London: Phaidon Press Ltd. Text volume, 1–126, 14 unnumbered pages, 178 figures. Catalogue volume, 1–183, 13 unnumbered pages. Plate volume, 12 unnumbered pages, 168 plates.

La scultura italiana. Part 1, *Il Gotico.* Translation by Luisa Vertova Nicolson of the 1955 edition of *Italian Gothic Sculpture.* Milan: Giangiacomo Feltrinelli Editore. viii, 228 pages, 101 figures, 108 plates.

"Italian Bronze Statuettes." Parts 1, 2. *The Burlington Magazine* 105 (January, February): 14–23, 58–71.

"New Works by Giovanni Pisano—I." *The Burlington Magazine* 105 (December): 529–33. Part 2, "An Ivory by Giovanni Pisano," was published in the *Bulletin of the Victoria and Albert Museum,* July 1965.

"Identity and Attribute." Review of *Italian Pictures of the Renaissance: Florentine School* by Bernard Berenson. *The Times Literary Supplement,* September 13: 684.

"A Family Exhibition." Review of *Il tesoro dei Medici* by Antonio Morassi. *The Times Literary Supplement*, October 11: 805.

"Complicated Artist." Review of *Giovanni Bellini* by Rodolfo Pallucchini. *The Times Literary Supplement*, December 12: 1024.

"Talking of Angels: Michelangelo in His Letters." Review of *I, Michelangelo, Sculptor* translated by Charles Speroni and edited by Irving and Jean Stone. *The Times Literary Supplement*, August 2: 585–86.

1964

Catalogue of Italian Sculpture in the Victoria and Albert Museum, assisted by Ronald Lightbown. 3 volumes. London: Her Majesty's Stationery Office. Volume 1, *Eighth to Fifteenth Century*. xvi, 395 pages. Volume 2, *Sixteenth to Twentieth Century*. v, 396–767 pages. Volume 3, *Plates*. 736 figures on 426 plates.

La scultura italiana. Part 2, *Il Quattrocento*. Translation by Luisa Vertova Nicolson of the 1958 edition of *Italian Renaissance Sculpture*. Milan: Giangiacomo Feltrinelli Editore. viii, 363 pages, 165 figures, 144 plates.

"Bronze that Shows Cellini Experimenting." *The Times*, October 27: 13.

"The Italian Plaquette." *The Proceedings of the British Academy* 50: 1–85.

"Sculpture for the Victoria and Albert Museum." *Apollo* 80 (December): 458–65.

"Two Models for the Tomb of Michelangelo." In *Studien zur toskanischen Kunst: Festschrift für Ludwig Heinrich Heydenreich zum 23. März 1963*: 237–43. Munich: Prestel-Verlag.

"In the Duke's Study." Review of *Le Palais Ducal d'Urbin* by Jacques Lavalleye. *The Times Literary Supplement*, December 24: 1156.

"In the Queen's Museum." Review of *Canaletto Paintings in the Collection of Her Majesty the Queen* by Michael Levey. *The Times Literary Supplement*, December 24: 1156.

"Flemish Primitives." Review of *Les primitifs flamands. I. Corpus de la peinture des anciens Pays-Bas méridionaux au 15e siècle.* Volume 6, *La Chapelle Royale de Grenade* by Roger van Schoute. *The Times Literary Supplement*, April 23: 330.

"Miscellany of Monuments." Review of *Renaissance Sculpture* by Hans Weigert. *The Times Literary Supplement*, September 24: 872.

"Michelangelo Receives the Tributes He Deserves." Review of *The Letters of Michelangelo* translated and annotated by E. H. Ramsden, and *The Divine Michelangelo: The Florentine Academy's Homage on His Death in 1564*, a facsimile edition of *Esequie del divino Michelangelo Buonarroti*, Florence, 1564, translated and annotated by Rudolf and Margot Wittkower. *The Times Literary Supplement*, April 2: 268.

Introduction to *Renaissance Bronzes in American Collections: An Exhibition Organized by the Smith College Museum of Art.* Northampton, Massachusetts. 6 unnumbered pages.

"Mr. Julius Goldschmidt." Obituary tribute. *The Times*, December 1: 12.

1965

Complete Catalogue of the Samuel H. Kress Collection. Renaissance Bronzes: Reliefs, Plaquettes, Statuettes, Utensils, and Mortars. London: Phaidon Press Ltd. viii, 1–160, 323–35 pages, 616 illustrations on 157 plates.

"The Contribution of Museums to Scholarship." In *Papers from the Seventh General Conference of ICOM* (International Council of Museums): 31–43. New York: The Metropolitan Museum of Art.

"An Ivory by Giovanni Pisano." *Victoria and Albert Museum Bulletin* 1 (July): 9–16.

"Portrait Sculptures by Ridolfo Sirigatti." *Victoria and Albert Museum Bulletin* 1 (April): 33–36.

"A Sketch-Model by Benvenuto Cellini." *Victoria and Albert Museum Bulletin* 1 (January): 5–9.

"Giorgione Question Marks." Review of *Giorgione* by Ludwig Baldass. *The Times Literary Supplement*, December 9: 1120.

"Painting for the Pope." Review of *The Sistine Chapel Before Michelangelo* by L. D. Ettlinger. *The Times Literary Supplement*, December 9: 1120.

"Italians in the Szepmuveszeti." Review of *North Italian Drawings from the Collection of the Budapest Museum of Fine Arts* by Iván Fenyö. *The Times Literary Supplement*, December 23: 1192.

"*Die Düsseldorfer Skizzenbücher des Guglielmo della Porta* by Werner Gramberg." *Master Drawings* 3 (December): 281–82.

"A Fountain in Siena." Review of *Jacopo della Quercia's Fonte gaia* by Anne Coffin Hanson. *The Times Literary Supplement*, April 1: 248.

"In Blinding Colour." Review of *Italian Drawings and Paintings in The Queen's Collection* edited by Oliver Millar. *The Times Literary Supplement*, March 4: 160.

"Brave Colours but Cowardly Form." Review of *Andrea del Sarto* by John Shearman. *The Times Literary Supplement*, April 22: 306.

"In Private and Public." Review of *The Drawings of Pontormo* by Janet Cox Rearick, and *The Chapel of the Cardinal of Portugal, 1434–1459, at San Miniato in Florence* by Frederick Hartt, Gino Corti, and Clarence Kennedy. *The Times Literary Supplement*, May 13: 364.

1966

Florence: What Has Happened and What Can Be Done—A Report. London: The Italian Art and Archives Rescue Fund. 12 unnumbered pages. Brochure based on text of article in *The Financial Times.*

The Portrait in the Renaissance. The A. W. Mellon Lectures in the Fine Arts, no. 12; Bollingen series, no. 35. New York: Bollingen Foundation. xxxii, 348 pages, 330 illustrations. Lectures delivered at the National Gallery of Art, Washington, D.C., 1963.

The Raphael Cartoons. Reprint of 1950 edition. Victoria and Albert Museum Colour Book no. 1. London: Her Majesty's Stationery Office. 10 pages, 30 plates (7 color).

La scultura italiana. Part 3, *Il Cinquecento e il Barocco.* Translation by Luisa Vertova Nicolson of the 1963 edition of *Italian High Renaissance and Baroque Sculpture.* 2 volumes. Milan: Giangiacomo Feltrinelli Editore. Text volume: 128 pages, 178 figures. Plate volume: 8 unnumbered pages, a catalogue section which is paginated 301–466, 168 plates.

"Antonio Calcagni's Bust of Annibale Caro." In *Arte in Europa: Scritti di storia dell'arte in onore di Edoardo Arslan*: 577–80. Milan: Artipo.

"Florence: What Has Happened and What Can Be Done." *The Financial Times,* November 25: 9.

"A New Work by Giovanni Bologna." *Victoria and Albert Museum Bulletin* 2 (April): 75–77.

"Quatre sculptures de la Renaissance au Victoria and Albert Museum de Londres." *L'information d'histoire de l'art* 11 (March–April): 66–78.

"Renaissance Drawings." Review of the exhibition catalogue *Drawings from New York Collections.* Volume 1, *The Italian Ren-*

aissance by Jacob Bean and Felice Stampfle. *The Times Literary Supplement*, February 10: 96.

"Writing Down Florence." Review of *The Companion Guide to Florence* by Eve Borsook. *The Times Literary Supplement*, July 21: 630.

"Round and Too Rosy." Review of *Donatello* by Giorgio Castelfranco. *The Times Literary Supplement*, January 27: 56.

"Officina italiana." Review of *The Studios and Styles of the Renaissance: Italy, 1460–1500* by André Chastel. *The Times Literary Supplement*, July 28: 674.

"Getting at Rembrandt." Review of *Rembrandt and the Italian Renaissance* by Kenneth Clark. *The New York Review of Books*, September 8: 22–23.

"What Pisanello Did." Review of *I disegni del Pisanello e della sua cerchia* by Maria Fossi Todorow. *The Times Literary Supplement*, October 27: 986.

"Michelangelo in Part." Review of *The Paintings of Michelangelo* by Frederick Hartt. *The Times Literary Supplement*, February 3: 76.

"Bernini's Sculptures." Review of *Bernini* by Howard Hibbard. *The Times Literary Supplement*, February 10: 96.

"De Sanctis Depinctis." Review of *Iconography of the Saints in Central and South Italian Schools of Painting* by George Kaftal. *The Times Literary Supplement*, March 31: 270.

"Berenson in a Landscape." Review of *Forty Years with Berenson* by Nicky Mariano. *The Times Literary Supplement*, July 7: 591.

"Fourteenth-Century Venetian Painting." Review of *La pittura veneziana del Trecento* by Rudolfo Pallucchini. *The Times Literary Supplement*, February 10: 96.

"Sienese Stylist." Review of *Taddeo di Bartolo* by Sibilla Symeonides. *The Times Literary Supplement*, April 28: 360.

1967

"Antonio Calcagni's Bust of Annibale Caro." *Victoria and Albert Museum Bulletin* 3 (January): 13–17. Reprinted from the Arslan *Festschrift*, 1966.

"Devastation of Florence." *Apollo* 85 (February): 130–32.

"Florenz—was geschehen ist und was getan werden kann—ein Bericht." *Kunstchronik* 20 (July): 177–83. Reprinted from *The Financial Times*, November 25, 1966.

"Foggini and Soldani: Some Recent Acquisitions." *Victoria and Albert Museum Bulletin* 3 (October): 135–44.

"The Palestrina Pietà." In *Stil und Überlieferung in der Kunst des Abendlandes*. Volume 2, *Michelangelo*: 105–14. Acts of the 21st Congress for the History of Art, Bonn, 1964. Berlin: Gebr. Mann Publishers.

"Three Marble Reliefs in the Gambier-Parry Collection." *The Burlington Magazine* 109 (March): 117–21.

"The Post-Raphaelites." Review of *A Failure of Nerve: Italian Painting, 1520–1535* by Kenneth Clark. *The Times Literary Supplement*, December 28: 1252.

"Early Dutch." Review of *Early Netherlandish Painting*. Volume I, *The van Eycks-Petrus Christus* by Max J. Friedländer. *The Times Literary Supplement*, July 6: 592.

"Art in Rome." Review of *Kunstgeschichtliche Studien zu Renaissance und Barock* by Jacob Hess. *The Times Literary Supplement*, October 19: 976.

"Antwerp Mannerist." Review of *La Renaissance flamande: Pieter Coeck d'Alost* by Georges Marlier. *The Times Literary Supplement*, March 30: 260.

"The Parmesan School." Review of *Italian Drawings in the Department of Prints and Drawings in the British Museum: Artists Working in Parma in the Sixteenth Century* by A. E. Popham. *The Times Literary Supplement,* August 31: 776.

"Florentine Galleries." Review of *The Uffizi and Pitti* by Filippo Rossi. *The Times Literary Supplement,* March 16: 212.

"All about Michelangelo." Review of *The Complete Work of Michelangelo* compiled under the direction of Mario Salmi. *The Times Literary Supplement,* February 2: 82.

"Mustered by Kress." Review of *Paintings from the Samuel H. Kress Collection: Italian Schools XIII–XV Century* by Fern Rusk Shapley. *The Times Literary Supplement,* January 19: 40.

"Making Up Their Moods." Review of *The Vision of Landscape in Renaissance Italy* by A. Richard Turner. *The Times Literary Supplement,* March 30: 260.

"Two and a Half Centuries of European Art." Review of *Sculpture in the Netherlands, Germany, France and Spain, 1400–1500* by Theodor Müller, and *Art and Architecture in Italy, 1250 to 1400* by John White. *The Times Literary Supplement,* February 2: 82.

Consultant editor for *A History of Western Sculpture.* Volume 1, *Classical Sculpture* by George M. A. Hanfmann. Volume 2, *Medieval Sculpture* by Roberto Salvini. Volume 3, *Sculpture: Renaissance to Roccoco* by Herbert Keutner. Volume 4, *Sculpture: 19th & 20th Centuries* by Fred Licht. London: George Rainbird Ltd., 1967–69.

1968

Essays on Italian Sculpture. A collection of twenty-five essays with a foreword and a postscript; they include "New Works by Giovanni Pisano—I" reprinted from *The Burlington Magazine,* 1963, "New Works by Giovanni Pisano—II" reprinted from the *Bulletin of the Victoria and Albert Museum,* 1965, "The Arca of St. Dominic: A Hypothesis" reprinted from *The Burlington Magazine,* 1951, "Notes on a Florentine Tomb Front" reprinted from *The Burlington Magazine*, 1949, "The Fifth Centenary of Donatello," a lecture delivered at the Victoria and Albert Museum on December 13, 1966, "Donatello's Relief of the Ascension" reprinted from a Victoria and Albert Museum monograph, 1949, "Some Donatello Problems" reprinted from *Studies in the History of Art Dedicated to William E. Suida*, 1959, "The Martelli David" reprinted from *The Burlington Magazine*, 1959, "The Virgin with the Laughing Child" reprinted from a Victoria and Albert Museum monograph, 1949, "A Relief by Agostino di Duccio" reprinted from a Victoria and Albert Museum monograph, 1952, "Two Paduan Bronzes" reprinted from *The Burlington Magazine*, 1954, "Two Chimney-Pieces from Padua" reprinted from *Arte antica e moderna*, 1961, "A Relief by Sansovino" reprinted from *The Burlington Magazine*, 1959, "Michelangelo in His Letters" reprinted from *The Times Literary Supplement*, 1963, "Michelangelo's Cupid: The End of a Chapter" reprinted from *The Burlington Magazine*, 1956, "The Palestrina Pietà" reprinted from *Stil und Überlieferung in der Kunst des Abendlandes*, 1967, "Two Models for the Tomb of Michelangelo" reprinted from *Studien zur toskanischen Kunst*, 1964, "A Small Bronze by Tribolo" reprinted from *The Burlington Magazine*, 1959, "A Sketch-Model by Benvenuto Cellini" reprinted from the *Victoria and Albert Museum Bulletin*, 1965, "Giovanni Bologna's Samson and a Philistine" reprinted from a Victoria and Albert Museum monograph, 1954, "Antonio Calcagni's Bust of Annibale Caro" reprinted from *Arte in Europa*, 1966, "Portrait Sculptures by Ridolfo Sirigatti" reprinted from the *Victoria and Albert Museum Bulletin*, 1965, "Some Bronze Statuettes by Francesco Fanelli" reprinted from *The Burlington Magazine*, 1953, "An Exhibition of Italian Bronze Statuettes" reprinted from *The Burlington Magazine*, 1963, "Portrait of an Art Historian" reprinted from *The Times Literary Supplement*, 1960. London and New York: Phaidon Press Ltd. i–ix, 243 pages, 248 illustrations.

"Two Veronese Angels." In *Festschrift Ulrich Middeldorf*: 39–41. Berlin: Walter de Gruyter & Co.

"Changing Painting." Review of *Masaccio* by Luciano Berti. *The Times Literary Supplement*, November 7: 1246.

"Italians in Cambridge." Review of *Fitzwilliam Museum, Cambridge: Catalogue of Paintings*. Volume 2, *Italian Schools* by J. W. Goodison and G. H. Robertson. *The Times Literary Supplement*, February 22: 172.

"Treasures of the Hermitage." Review of *The Hermitage, Leningrad: Medieval and Renaissance Masters* with an introduction by V. F. Levinson-Lessing and notes by the staff of the Hermitage. *The Times Literary Supplement*, January 11: 28.

"Giovanni, Son of Jacopo." Review of *Giovanni Bellini* by Giles Robertson. *The Times Literary Supplement*, December 26: 1453.

Foreword to *Musical Instruments as Works of Art*. Victoria and Albert Museum Large Special Miscellaneous Publications no. 10. London: Her Majesty's Stationery Office. 1 unnumbered page.

Foreword to *Victoria and Albert Museum: Catalogue of Musical Instruments*. Volume 1, *Keyboard Instruments* by Raymond Russell: vii–viii. London: Her Majesty's Stationery Office.

Foreword to *Victoria and Albert Museum: Catalogue of Musical Instruments*. Volume 2, *Non-keyboard Instruments* by Anthony Baines: vii. London: Her Majesty's Stationery Office.

1969

Preface to the catalogue *Frescoes from Florence*: 13–14. London: The Arts Council.

Paolo Uccello: Complete Edition. Second, revised edition of 1950 monograph. London and New York: Phaidon Press Ltd. vii, 1–28, 139–88 pages, color frontispiece, 19 figures, 112 plates (6 color).

"The Interaction of Painting and Sculpture in Florence in the

Fifteenth Century." The Selwyn Brinton Lecture, read on February 26, 1969. *The Journal of the Royal Society of Arts* 117 (May): 406–24.

"Specimens or People: Some Problems for Art Museums." *Museums Journal* 69 (December): 106–7.

"Writing on Art." *Essays by Divers Hands* 35: 101–14. The Nicholas Gifford Edmonds Memorial Lecture, read on June 24, 1966.

"Scottish Italians." Review of *National Gallery of Scotland: Catalogue of Italian Drawings* by Keith Andrews. *The Times Literary Supplement*, January 16: 54

"Illustrating Berenson's Precepts." Review of *Italian Pictures of the Renaissance: Central Italian and North Italian Schools* by Bernard Berenson. *The Times Literary Supplement*, January 2: 9.

"The 'Aemulus' of Donatello." Review of *Verrocchio* by Gunther Passavant. *The Times Literary Supplement*, November 13: 1296.

"Above the Doge's Head." Review of *Venetian Painted Ceilings of the Renaissance* by Juergen Schulz. *The Times Literary Supplement*, December 18: 1440.

Acknowledgments in the exhibition catalogue *Berlioz and the Romantic Imagination*: vii–viii. London: The Arts Council.

Foreword to *Victoria and Albert Museum: Designs for English Sculpture, 1680–1860* by John Physick: v. London: Her Majesty's Stationery Office.

Foreword to *Victoria and Albert Museum: English Watches* by J. F. Hayward. London: Her Majesty's Stationery Office. 1 unnumbered page.

Foreword to the *Victoria and Albert Museum Yearbook* 1: vii.

1970

The Frick Collection: An Illustrated Catalogue. Volume 3, *Sculpture: Italian*, assisted by Anthony F. Radcliffe. New York: The Frick

Collection. xxv–xxxii, 254 pages, color frontispiece, 114 black-and-white illustrations, 7 color plates. Volume 4, *Sculpture: German, Netherlandish, French, and British*, assisted by Anthony F. Radcliffe; the 18th- and 19th-century French and British entries by Terrence W. I. Hodgkinson. New York: The Frick Collection. 3–68 pages, color frontispiece, 40 black-and-white illustrations, 2 color plates.

An Introduction to Italian Sculpture. Part 3. *Italian High Renaissance and Baroque Sculpture.* Second, revised edition of book published in 1963. London and New York: Phaidon Press Ltd. 1–126, 299–468, 16 unnumbered pages, 178 figures, 168 plates.

Raphael. London: Phaidon Press Ltd. 304 pages, frontispiece, 246 illustrations including 6 color plates. The Wrightsman Lectures delivered in 1965 under the auspices of the New York University Institute of Fine Arts.

"The Altman Madonna by Antonio Rossellino." *Metropolitan Museum Journal* 3: 133–48.

"The Gherardini Collection of Italian Sculpture." *Victoria and Albert Museum Yearbook* 2: 7–26.

"Giovanni Bologna and the Marble Statues of the Grand-Duke Ferdinand I." *The Burlington Magazine* 112 (May): 304–7.

"Berenson in an Expansionist Trough." Review of *Homeless Paintings of the Renaissance* by Bernard Berenson. *The Times Literary Supplement*, January 29: 100.

"Suspicious Glances towards Raphael." Review of *Raphael* by A. P. Oppe, edited by Charles Mitchell. *The Times Literary Supplement*, October 30: 1243.

"Leonardo Re-catalogued." Review of *The Drawings of Leonardo da Vinci in the Collection of Her Majesty The Queen at Windsor Castle* by Kenneth Clark, revised with the assistance of Carlo Pedretti, and *Leonardo's Legacy* edited by C. D. O'Malley. *The Times Literary Supplement*, January 15: 48.

"Empirical Master of the High Renaissance." Review of *The*

Paintings of Titian. Volume 1, *The Religious Paintings* by Harold Wethey, and *Problems in Titian, Mostly Iconographic* by Erwin Panofsky. *The Times Literary Supplement*, June 4: 600.

"Raphael." Reply to a letter from Charles Mitchell. *The Times Literary Supplement*, December 11: 1466.

1971

An Introduction to Italian Sculpture. Part 2. *Italian Renaissance Sculpture*. Second, revised edition of book published in 1958. London and New York: Phaidon Press Ltd. 2–96, 246–365, 17 unnumbered pages, 165 figures, 144 plates.

"Cataloguing the Frick Bronzes." *Apollo* 93 (May): 366–73.

"Drawing." Review of the exhibition catalogue *Drawings from New York Collections*. Volume 3, *The Eighteenth Century in Italy* by Jacob Bean and Felice Stampfle. *The Times Literary Supplement*, July 2: 760.

"Early Flemish." Review of *Les primitifs flamands. I. Corpus de la peinture des anciens Pays-Bas méridionaux au 15e siècle*. Volume 11, *The National Gallery, London* by Martin Davies. *The Times Literary Supplement*, February 26: 237.

"What Did Raphael Paint?" Review of *Raphael* by Luitpold Dussler. *The Times Literary Supplement*, June 11: 668.

"The Pattern of the Cinquecento." Review of *Painting in Italy, 1500–1600* by S. J. Freedberg. *The Times Literary Supplement*, October 22: 1304.

"Septuagenary Feast." Review of *Studies in Early Christian, Medieval, and Renaissance Art* by Richard Krautheimer. *The Times Literary Supplement*, September 19: 1104.

"Venice's Trecento Master." Review of *Paolo da Venezia* by Michelangelo Muraro. *The Times Literary Supplement*, September 24: 1142.

"The Unproductive Master of Venice: Additions and Subtractions in the Giorgione Catalogue." Review of *Giorgione* by Terisio Pignatti. *The Times Literary Supplement*, April 30: 503–4.

1972

An Introduction to Italian Sculpture. Part 1. Italian Gothic Sculpture. Second, substantially revised edition of book published in 1955. London and New York: Phaidon Press Ltd. 1–51, 170–222, 276–284, 22 unnumbered pages, 93 figures, 112 plates.

"The Tombs and Monuments." A chapter in *Westminster Abbey*: 197–254. Radnor, Pennsylvania: Annenberg School Press. 47 illustrations (4 color), 6 diagrams.

"A Poetic Master of the Seicento." Review of *Pier Francesco Mola* by Richard Cocke. *The Times Literary Supplement*, May 5: 508.

"Truly van Eyck." Review of *Les primitifs flamands. I. Corpus de la peinture des anciens Pays-Bas méridionaux au 15e siècle.* Volume 12, *The National Gallery of Victoria, Melbourne* by Ursula Hoff and Martin Davies. *The Times Literary Supplement*, May 12: 542.

"Portal Remains." Review of *Ghiberti's Bronze Doors* by Richard Krautheimer. *The Times Literary Supplement*, June 2: 620.

"Memling Restored." Review of *Hans Memling* by K. B. McFarlane. *The Times Literary Supplement*, March 17: 294.

"Rehabilitating an Eclectic." Review of *Annibale Carracci* by Donald Posner. *The Times Literary Supplement*, September 22: 1103–4.

"The Unquestioned Superiority of Titian." Review of *The Paintings of Titian. Volume 2, The Portraits* by Harold E. Wethey. *The Times Literary Supplement*, February 25: 222.

Foreword to the catalogue for the 14th exhibition of the Council of Europe *The Age of Neo-Classicism*: xii–xvi. London: The Arts Council of Great Britain.

1973

"Italy in America." Review of *Paintings from the Samuel H. Kress Collection: Italian Schools XVI–XVIII Century* by Fern Rusk Shapley. *The Times Literary Supplement*, August 17: 944.

1974

Fra Angelico. Second, amplified edition of the 1952 monograph. London: Phaidon Press Ltd.; Ithaca, New York: Cornell University Press. vi, 1–40, 188–242 pages, color frontispiece, 117 figures, 14 color plates, 143 black-and-white plates.

"The Forging of Italian Renaissance Sculpture." *Apollo* 99 (April): 242–67.

"The Man Who Put Things in the Round." An essay on Masaccio. *Observer Magazine*, September 15: 32–36.

"Some Newly Acquired Italian Sculptures: A Relief of the Rape of Europa, a Fountain by Rustici, a Portrait Sketch Model by Algardi." *Victoria and Albert Museum Yearbook* 4: 11–47.

"Shots of Donatello." Review of *Donatello: Prophet of Modern Vision* by David Finn and Frederick Hartt. *The New York Review of Books*, January 24: 7–9.

1975

"Design in Museums." *Journal of the Royal Society of Arts* 123 (October): 717–27.

"Interaction between National and Regional Museums." *Museums Journal* 75 (December): 110–13.

"The Medici Crucifixion of Donatello." *Apollo* 101 (February): 82–87.

"Michelangelo: The Fruits of Age." *The Sunday Times*, February 9: 8–15.

"The Painting in My Life." An essay on Titian's *The Three Ages of Man*. *The Sunday Times*, September 28: 48–49.

"*Vecchietta and the Sacristy of the Siena Hospital Church: A Study in Renaissance Religious Symbolism* by H. W. van Os." *Apollo* 101 (June): 495–96.

"The Modernity of Titian." Review of *Titian: The Mythological and Historical Paintings* by Harold E. Wethey. *The Times Literary Supplement*, August 15: 910.

"Italian Sculpture—Budapest and Paris." Review of *Katalog der ausländischen Bildwerke des Museums der Bildenden Künste in Budapest* by Jolán Balogh, *Inventaire des collections publiques françaises. Paris, Musée Jacquemart-André: Sculpture italienne* by Françoise de la Moureyre-Gavoty, and *Comune di Ferrara: Placchette e bronzi nelle civiche collezioni* by Ranieri Varese. *Apollo* 102 (December): 474–75.

"Considerations on Venetian Art." Review of *Venetian Art from Bellini to Titian* by Johannes Wilde and *Jacopo Sansovino* by Deborah Howard. *Apollo* 102 (September): 226–29.

Millard Meiss, 1904–1975. Address at memorial service, Princeton University Chapel, November 8, 1975: 12–14. Privately printed.

1976

Portretul in Renastere. Translation by Alexandra Dobrota of the Mellon Lectures first published in 1966. Bucharest: Editura Meridiane. 222 pages.

"The Madonna Reliefs of Donatello." *Apollo* 103 (March): 172–91.

"The Museum as Forum." *Expedition* 18 (Summer): 3–10.

"Critical Confrontations." Review of *Looking at Pictures with Bernard Berenson* compiled by Hanna Kiel. *The Times Literary Supplement*, May 28: 640.

"The Campagna Collection at Avignon." Review of *Avignon, Musée du Petit Palais: Peinture italienne* by Michel Laclotte and Elisabeth Mognetti. *Apollo* 104 (December): 518–19.

"*Holzkruzifixe in Florenz und in der Toskana von der Zeit um 1300 bis zum frühen Cinquecento* by Margrit Lisner." *Pantheon* 34 (January–March): 78–80.

"A Quota of Masterpieces." Review of *Complete Catalogue of the Samuel H. Kress Collection: European Sculptures, XIV–XIX Century* by Ulrich Middeldorf. *Apollo* 104 (July): 70–72.

"*What Is Art History?* by Mark Roskill." *The Times Literary Supplement*, August 6: 976.

"A Major Contribution to the Study of Italian Art." Review of *Italian Paintings in the Walters Art Gallery* by Federico Zeri. *Apollo* 104 (September): 229–30.

Foreword to *The British Museum Yearbook* 1: i.

Introduction to *British Museum Guide*: 7–8. London: British Museum Publications Ltd.

"Millard Meiss: In Memoriam." *The Art Journal* 35 (Spring): 262. Partial reprinting of memorial address delivered in 1975.

"James Pope-Hennessy." Letter concerning Alastair Forbes's remarks about James Pope-Hennessy. *The Times Literary Supplement*, October 29: 1363.

1977

"Donatello and the Bronze Statuette." *Apollo* 105 (January): 30–33.

"The Evangelist Roundels in the Pazzi Chapel." *Apollo* 106 (October): 262–69.

"*Giotto and Florentine Painting, 1280–1375* by Bruce Cole." *Apollo* 106 (September): 251–52.

"Completing the Account." Review of *Paintings from the Samuel H. Kress Collection: European Schools Excluding Italian* by Colin Eisler. *The Times Literary Supplement*, June 17: 726.

"Correggio Revalued." Review of *The Paintings of Correggio* by Cecil Gould. *Apollo* 106 (August): 157–58.

"*A Catalogue of the Earlier Italian Paintings in the Ashmolean Museum* by Christopher Lloyd." *Apollo* 106 (October): 319.

"The Rhetorician of Space." Review of *Botticelli* by L. D. and Helen S. Ettlinger, *Botticelli's Uffizi "Adoration": A Study in Pictorial Content* by Rab Hatfield, and *The Drawings by Sandro Botticelli for Dante's Divine Comedy* by Kenneth Clark. *The Times Literary Supplement*, February 18: 175.

"Depiction of Light." Review of *The Painter's Choice* by Millard Meiss and *The Heritage of Apelles* by E. H. Gombrich. *The New York Times Book Review*, May 8: 36–37.

1978

"The Branchini Madonna by Giovanni di Paolo." In *Art at Auction: The Year at Sotheby Parke Bernet, 1977–78*: 18–21. London and Totowa, New Jersey: Sotheby Parke Bernet Publications Ltd.

"The Branchini Madonna by Giovanni di Paolo." In *Masterpieces from The Robert von Hirsh Sale at Sotheby's with an Article on the Branchini Madonna by Sir John Pope-Hennessy*: 9–11. Westerham, Kent: Westerham Press Ltd. Reprinted from *Art at Auction*, 1978.

"Gothic Sculpture in Venice." Review of *La scultura veneziana gothica, 1300–1460* by Wolfgang Walters. *Apollo* 108 (July): 74–75.

1979

The Portrait in the Renaissance. Paperback edition of the Mellon Lectures first published in 1966. Bollingen Series, no. 35. Princeton, New Jersey: Princeton University Press. xxxii, 348 pages, 330 illustrations.

Raphael. Paperback edition of the book published in 1970. New York, Hagerstown, San Francisco, and London: Harper & Row, Publishers. 304 pages, frontispiece, 246 plates.

"The Ford Italian Paintings." *Bulletin of The Detroit Institute of Arts* 57: 14–23.

"Thoughts on Andrea della Robbia." *Apollo* 109 (March): 176–97.

"A Revolutionary Artist." Review of *Antonio and Piero Pollaiuolo: Complete Edition with a Critical Catalogue* by Leopold D. Ettlinger. *The New York Review of Books*, March 8: 39–40.

"Sienese Painting and the *Paragonisti*." Review of *La Pinacoteca Nazionale di Siena: I dipinti dal XII al XV secolo* by Piero Torriti. *Apollo* 109 (April): 325–26.

"Entrepreneur of the Renaissance." Review of *Giorgio Vasari: The Man and the Book* by T. S. R. Boase, and *Lives of the Most Eminent Painters, Sculptors, and Architects* by Giorgio Vasari translated by Gaston Du C. de Vere, introduction by Kenneth Clark. *The Washington Post Bookworld*, October 21: 5.

Foreword to *The Martin D'Arcy Gallery of Art. The First Ten Years: Notable Acquisitions of Medieval, Renaissance, and Baroque Art.* Chicago: Loyola University of Chicago. 1 unnumbered page.

"Meyer Shapiro Honored." An address honoring Meyer Shapiro when he received the Jan Mitchell Prize for Art History, November 7, 1979. *Art/World*, November 17–December 15: 1, 14.

1980

Luca della Robbia. Oxford: Phaidon Press Ltd.; distributed in the United States by Cornell University Press. 1–93, 225–28 pages, 66 figures, 32 color plates, 128 black-and-white plates.

The Study and Criticism of Italian Sculpture. A collection of ten essays with a preface and postscript; they include "Connoisseurship" and "The Sixth Centenary of Ghiberti" both published here for the first time, "The Italian Plaquette" reprinted from the *Proceedings of the British Academy*, 1964, "The Altman Madonna by Antonio Rossellino" reprinted from the *Metropolitan Museum Journal*, 1970, and the following articles published in *Apollo* between 1974 and 1979: "The Forging of Italian Renaissance Sculpture," "The Medici Crucifixion of Donatello," "The Madonna Reliefs of Donatello," "Donatello and the Bronze Statuette," "The Evangelist Roundels in the Pazzi Chapel", and "Thoughts on Andrea della Robbia." New York: The Metropolitan Museum of Art. 270 pages, 244 illustrations.

"The International Heritage." In *The Preservation and Use of Artistic Cultural Heritage: Perspectives and Solutions*: 164–76. New York: The Metropolitan Museum of Art.

"The Relations between Florentine and Venetian Sculpture in the Sixteenth Century." In *Florence and Venice: Comparisons and Relations*. Volume 2: 323–35. Florence: La Nuova Italia Editrice.

"Secular Painting in 15th-Century Tuscany: Birth Trays, Cassone Panels, and Portraits," in collaboration with Keith Christiansen. *The Metropolitan Museum of Art Bulletin* 38 (Summer): 2–64.

"A Blurred View of Berenson." Review of *Being Bernard Berenson* by Meryle Secrest. *Now!* January 18: 70–72.

"A Misfit Master." Review of *Duccio: Tuscan Art and the Medieval Workshop* by John White and *Duccio di Buoninsegna and His School* by James H. Stubblebine. *The New York Review of Books*, November 20: 45–47.

Introduction to the reprinted edition of *Botticelli: Painter of Florence* by Herbert P. Horne: ix–xiii. Princeton, New Jersey: Princeton University Press.

Preface to *Italian Paintings: A Catalogue of the Collection of The Metropolitan Museum of Art, Sienese and Central Italian Schools* by Federico Zeri with the assistance of Elizabeth E. Gardner: ix. New York: The Metropolitan Museum of Art.

"The Case of Luca della Robbia." Letter in response to a review by H. W. Janson. *The New York Review of Books*, May 1: 44–45.

1981

Angelico. A trilingual edition of the introduction to the 1974 revision of *Fra Angelico*; French translation by Fabrice Gaugier, Italian by Mirella Manchilli-Billi, Spanish by Virginia Vezzoso. Florence: Becocci Editore. 80 pages, 88 color plates.

A Kingdom of Flowers. Calendar for 1982. New York: The Metropolitan Museum of Art. 3 unnumbered pages.

1982

"A Bronze Satyr by Cellini." *The Burlington Magazine* 124 (July): 406–12.

"A Shocking Scene." Essay on a pavement in the Siena cathedral traditionally attributed to Matteo di Giovanni. *Apollo* 115 (March): 150–57.

"Il Gotico a Siena." Review of the exhibition at the Palazzo Pubblico, Siena. *The Burlington Magazine* 124 (November): 716–19.

"A Museum Marks Its First 400 Years." Review of the exhibition La Città degli Uffizi at Florence. *The New York Times*, Sunday Arts and Leisure Section, June 23: 1, 26.

Preface to *Hebrew Illuminated Manuscripts in the British Isles* by Bezalel Narkiss: 7–8. Jerusalem and London: The Israel Academy of Sciences and Humanities, and The British Academy.

Creatures of Heaven and Earth. Calendar for 1983. New York: The Metropolitan Museum of Art. 3 unnumbered pages.

"Interview with Sir John Pope-Hennessy," by Susan J. Cooperman and David Levy. *The Rutgers Art Review* 3 (January): 97–104.

1983

Raffaello. Translation by Elda Negri Monateri of the Wrightsman Lectures first published in 1970, with a new introduction. Turin: Umberto Allemandi & C. 164 pages, 41 illustrations.

"Die Maler von Siena." A collection of five essays on Sienese painting entitled "*Sena Vetus*," "*Civitas Virginis*," "Die Landschaft in der Malerei Sienas," "Szenen aus dem Alltagsleben," and "Siena und seine Klosterkirchen," translated by Jörg Trobitius. *Du: Die Kunstzeitschrift* May: 26–65.

"A Terracotta 'Madonna' by Donatello." *The Burlington Magazine* 125 (February): 83–85.

"A Humanist's Vision." Review of *The Art of Humanism* by Kenneth Clark. *Apollo* 119 (February): 145.

"The Sensuous and the Cerebral." Review of *Domenichino* by Richard E. Spear. *The Times Literary Supplement*, March 25: 305.

"Centenary of a Cipher." Review of *Raphael Vrbinas: Il mito della Fornarina* edited by Dante Bernini, *Raphael in der Alten Pinakothek* by Hubertus von Sonnenburg, *The Drawings of Raphael* by Paul Joannides, *Raffaello* by Konrad Oberhuber, and *Raphael* by Roger Jones and Nicholas Penny. *The New York Review of Books*, December 22: 44–47.

Foreword to *Nicholas Hilliard's Art of Limning: A New Edition of a Treatise Concerning the Arte of Limning, Writ by N Hilliard* transcribed by Arthur F. Kinney, edited by Linda Bradley Salamon: xi–xii. Boston, Massachusetts: Northeastern University Press.

"Sir Leigh Ashton: Postwar Reorganization at the Victoria and Albert Museum." Obituary. *The Times*, March 17: 14.

"Professor Ulrich Middeldorf." Obituary. *Apollo* 117 (May): 420.

1984

"Donatello's Bronze David." In *Scritti di storia dell'arte in onore di Federico Zeri*, Volume 1: 122–27. Milan: Electa Editrice.

"Roger Fry and The Metropolitan Museum of Art." In *Oxford, China, and Italy: Writings in Honour of Sir Harold Acton on His Eightieth Birthday* edited by Edward Chaney and Neil Ritchie: 229–40. London: Thames and Hudson.

"A Humanist's Vision." Review of *The Art of Humanism* by Kenneth Clark. *Apollo* 119 (February): 145.

Foreword to Walter Liedtke's catalogue *Flemish Paintings in The Metropolitan Museum of Art*, Volume 1: ix. New York: The Metropolitan Museum of Art.

Introduction to *The Jack and Belle Linsky Collection in The Metropolitan Museum of Art*: 11–12. New York: The Metropolitan Museum of Art.

"Lord Clark of Saltwood." Address given at the memorial service for Lord Clark at St. James's Church, Piccadilly, October 13, 1983. *Apollo* 119 (January): 58–59.

"Spotlight: Sir John Pope-Hennessy." Address given at Art Dealers Association of America award dinner. *Update: A News Digest for ADAA Members* 3(Spring): 2–4.

1985

Cellini. New York: Abbeville Press. 324 pages, 103 figures, 155 plates (74 color). Published with same pagination and illustrations in a British edition, London: Macmillan, and a French edition translated by Dominique Le Bourg, Paris: Éditions F. Hazan.

An Introduction to Italian Sculpture. Paperback photo-offset copy of the second edition, 1970–72, with a new foreword, appendices and revised indices. New York and Toronto: Random House. Part 1, *Italian Gothic Sculpture.* 2–51, 170–222, 274–295, 19 unnumbered pages, 93 figures, 112 plates. Part 2, *Italian Renaissance Sculpture.* 2–96, 246–388, 25 unnumbered pages, 165 figures, 144 plates. Part 3, *Italian High Renaissance and Baroque Sculpture.* 1–126, 299–486, 14 unnumbered pages, 178 figures, 168 plates.

"Cellini." *Arts & Antiques*, November: 66–69.

"Cellini's Passion." *House & Garden*, December: 128–31, 206, 208–9, 212.

"Francesco Salviati: Portrait of a Young Man." Catalogue entry in *Liechtenstein: The Princely Collections*: 203–4. New York: The Metropolitan Museum of Art.

"The Healing Arts: The Loggia di San Paolo." *FMR*, January–February: 117–27.

"Leonardo: Landscape Painter." *Antaeus*, Spring: 41–54.

"Self-Portrait of an Art Historian as a Young Man." *The New York Times*, Sunday Arts and Leisure Section, December 8: 1, 39.

"Andrea Pisano and His Tuscan Contemporaries." Review of *Andrea Pisano und die toskanische Skulptur des 14. Jahrhunderts* by Gert Kreytenberg. *Apollo* 122 (August): 160–61.

"*A Corpus of Italian Medals Before Cellini* by George Francis Hill." Review of the reprint edited by J. G. Pollard. *The Medal* 7 (Winter): 55–56.

"The Right B. B." Letter identifying a remark Berenson made about Ivy Compton-Burnett. *The New York Review of Books*, March 14: 40.

"Mary M. Davis." Obituary. *The Burlington Magazine* 127 (July): 459.